BITTER GREENS

SUNY SERIES IN ITALIAN/AMERICAN CULTURE
Fred L. Gardaphe, editor

BITTER GREENS

**Essays on Food, Politics, and Ethnicity
from the Imperial Kitchen**

Anthony Di Renzo

excelsior editions

State University of New York Press
Albany, New York

GT
2853
. I58
D57
2010

Published by State University of New York Press, Albany

© 2010 State University of New York Press

Printed in the United States of America

Excelsior Editions is an imprint of State University of New York Press

For information, contact State University of New York Press, Albany, NY
www.sunypress.edu

Design by Cathleen Collins
Production by Dana Foote
Marketing by Fran Keneston

Library of Congress Cataloging-in-Publication Data

Di Renzo, Anthony, 1960–
  Bitter greens : essays on food, politics, and ethnicity from the imperial
kitchen / Anthony Di Renzo.
    p. cm. — (Suny series in Italian/American culture)
  ISBN 978-1-4384-3317-2 (hardcover : alk. paper)
  1. Food habits—Italy. 2. Food habits—United States. 3. Italian Americans—Food. 4. Cookery, Italian. 5. Italy—Social life and customs.
6. United States—Social life and customs. I. Title.
  GT2853.I58D57 2010
  641.30945–dc22
                          2009052825

10 9 8 7 6 5 4 3 2 1

For
Catherine Rankovic
Always Welcome at My Table

Si bene qui cenat bene vivit, lucet, eamus
quo ducit gula, piscemur, venemur, ut olim
Gargilius, qui mane plagas, venabula, servos
differtum transire forum populumque iubebat,
unus ut e multis populo spectante referret
emptum mulus aprum. Crudi tumidique lavemur,
quid deceat, quid non obliti, Caerite cera
digni, remigium vitiosum Ithacensis Ulixei,
cui potior patria fuit interdicta voluptas.

If eating well is living well, let's go! It's dawn!
Let's follow wherever our gullet leads!
Let's hunt and fish like that card Gargilius,
Who sent slaves through the Forum, with nets and spears,
So the crowd could gape at his store-bought boar slung on
     a mule like a trophy.
Stuffed like pigs, bellies bloated, let's wallow in the public
     baths—
Third-class citizens deaf to decency, depraved as Ulysses'
     scurvy crew,
Who preferred forbidden pleasure to their native land.
                              —Horace, *Epistles* I, 6

PROGRAM AND MENU

PREFACE

Aperitif

APERITIF

ROAST PEACOCK, Horace the Roman satirist assures us, tastes exactly like chicken. So does crow; properly seasoned, of course. Horace knew a hundred ways to prepare crow. While never as famished as the poor who clamored for grain in the forum, or were restrained from snatching the meat left on funeral pyres, Horace ate crow for thirty years. As a youth, he had fought with the Republicans at Philippi, but when the imperial forces broke the line, Horace discarded his shield and fled the battle. Pardoned by Octavian, the future Caesar Augustus, Horace became a secretary in the city treasury, attracted the patronage of Maecenas, and banqueted his way into Rome's literary circle. Good dining taught the country boy from Venusia, the freedman's son with the bad haircut, to chew and speak simultaneously and to talk out of both sides of his mouth. With these skills, Horace survived the new regime, published his poems, and was awarded a Sabine farm. That is the price of success: Sooner or later, we all eat our words.

Such a heavy meal demands an aperitif. Derived from the Latin *aperire*, aperitif literally means "opener." An aperitif opens a meal, just as a preface opens a book. It relaxes the nerves and stimulates the appetite. We Italians always have an *aperitivo* before supper and encourage our guests to join in. Shall I fetch some? Interestingly, this dinner custom began in the early Industrial Revolution. Originally medicine distilled from spices, herbs, roots, barks, and peels, *aperitivi* settled the digestive tract. Most contained diluted quinine, so wine was added to mellow the flavor. By the late nineteenth century, queasy from the shock of progress and plenty, the overwrought bourgeoisie of the Belle Époque inaugurated supper with an *aperitivo*, usually bitters. For true sophisticates, however, irony remains the aperitif of choice, especially when the entrée is humble pie.

My liquor cabinet is stocked with irony, different brands of irony. Some are harsh like Campari, others sour like Lemoncello, others semisweet like Cynar. Which would you prefer? I keep plenty on hand, since the fall of the Berlin Wall and the Twin Towers. For a lapsed socialist and a failed saint, who dreamed of writing for the *Catholic Worker*, the past twenty-five years have been a super-sizing of humble pie. I witnessed the triumph of global capitalism and the decline of the American Republic. But like Horace, I lost my shield at Philippi and learned to tolerate empire. After starving in the nonprofit sector, where malnutrition made my sweat stink like nail polish, I prostituted myself as a copywriter, publicist, and party hack; a period in my life I call the Babylonian Captivity. Repenting, I squandered my savings to earn a PhD, only to wind up teaching business and technical writing at a corporate college, the only academic job I could find in a brass-knuckled economy. Now I shop at the supermarket rather than the co-op, order from Amazon, not the downtown book store, and subscribe to ninety-five cable channels.

Vae victis! Woe to the vanquished. For consolation, I turn to Roman satire and Southern Italian cooking, two boons from my immigrant parents. Their Old World wisdom has taught me to outlive my New World illusions. Growing up, I often resented their unsolicited advice, especially during meals; but history has confirmed even their most cynical maxims. If I had heeded their table talk more, had been less of a glutton for punishment, I never would have eaten my heart out. Now reconciled, we enjoy each other's company, conversation, and cooking. Let me introduce you before dinner.

PAPA COMES FROM THE ABRUZZI, former stronghold of the Vestini, Paeligni, and Marsi and ancient home of *La Panarda*, a marathon feast in which guests must eat thirty courses or face the direst consequences. After nestling in the Apennines for five centuries, my relatives now live mostly in or near Rome. Homing instinct, I suspect, because our ancestors originated from Trastevere, Rome's raffish outlying district, located on the west bank of the Tiber and south of Vatican Hill. Back in Cicero's day, Trastevere was segregated from the rest of Rome. Only the rickety Pons

Sublicius connected the Urbs to this disreputable neighborhood, where the Cloaca Maxima discharged its sewage into the river. And fittingly so, sniffed the patricians, for the Trateverini were scum: fishermen, bargemen, and sailors who prized eels, caroused at Ostia, and mingled with Jews. To scandalize the establishment, Lady Clodia and Julius Caesar deliberately built their villas in Trastevere. The locals, they claimed, cooked the best food, cracked the best jokes, and threw the best block party. Ovid, another Abruzzese who settled in the capital, enjoyed this wide and wooly bash.

La Festa de' Noiantri still erupts every July, and my cousins Carla and Patrizia, both professors, attend for the street fritters and the public readings of Trastevere's two great dialect poets, Giuseppe Gioachino Belli and Trilussa, whose satires deal with the perpetual corruption of church and state and the eternal delight of Roman food. Their late father, Uncle Tonino, often recited these squibs at table, creating a counterpoint between formal literature and informal conversation. My father, more freewheeling and heavy-handed, prefers garnishing each dish with sarcasm and abuse; usually at my expense. As he explained to our guests one Thanksgiving: "I carve people, not birds." My mother, an expert with knives, blew him a kiss.

If Papa is Master of the Revels, Mamma is Queen of the Feast. A proud cook and a fierce debater, she hails from Sicily, the birthplace of Western rhetoric and the matrix of Mezzogiorno cuisine. Since the fourth century B.C., no one can talk or cook better than the Sicilians. They gabble as if they will live forever, and gobble as if they will never eat again. When Gorgias taught public speaking in Leontini, Mithraecus wrote the West's first cookbook and Labducus founded its first cooking school, in Syracuse. Neither could compete with Archestratus of Gela, whose refined pallet could taste the difference between a mullet caught during a waxing moon and a mullet caught during a waning moon. A freelance El Exigente, Archestratus toured the Mediterranean and rated the local fish market, giving tuna from Byzantium five stars but tuna from Cefalù only three.

Sicily, Mamma always reminds us, taught Rome how to eat. For the fat cats on the Palatine, owning a Sicilian chef became a status symbol: "*Siculus coquus et sicula mensa*," a Sicilian cook and a Sicilian table. This motto explains why smarmy Sicilian chefs so often appear in Roman satire. During a lavish dinner party, Trimalchio, the obnoxious billionaire of the *Satyricon*, tells his cook that he will add Sicily to his already vast estate, "so when I want to shop in Africa, I can sail there without ever leaving my backyard." Such decadence would have appalled Plato, who held Sicilians in contempt. After visiting the court of Dionysus the Tyrant, he concluded that Sicilian chefs threatened political freedom as much as Sicilian Sophists. Both spoiled and seduced the masses—the first with food, the second with words—and sowed the seeds of chaos and corruption.

Having seen prosperity rot a nation, I sympathize with Plato. Mamma, however, will have none of it. "That old windbag!" she snaps. "What does he know? He couldn't cook worth a damn!" She has a point. Plato's high dudgeon springs from a low opinion of the flesh. Before the eternal scandal of the tongue and belly, philosophy can only splutter; but the gut has its reasons of which reason knows not. Politics and religion, I've learned to my chagrin, always split on the reef of appetite. Consider my favorite passage from the Gospel of Saint Luke: "*Blessed are those who hunger and thirst for justice.*" When I recited this beatitude at my Confirmation dinner, my parents smiled and shook their heads. Beautiful words, they said, but don't take them too seriously. People hunger for justice as long as it remains a regular menu item. Some persist if it appears as an occasional early bird special. But once the kitchen closes, we take our hunger elsewhere. We substitute happiness for justice and, like actors in a margarine commercial, swear it's as yummy as butter.

WHETHER OR NOT I STILL HUNGER for justice, I spend most of my spare time cooking, a last refuge in an increasingly menacing world. When I am frisked at Newark Airport because I am mistaken for a Tunisian suspect, when I am grilled by campus security because I sent a flamer about a botched upgrade to computer support, when I am bullied in the Barnes & Noble parking lot because I bought a French novel and drive a Honda Civic, I retreat to the kitchen and make comfort food. Sometimes I read

Horace as I prepare dinner, but if I'm too brain-dead after a sixty-hour work week, I watch the Food Network instead. What spectacle! With a dash of tabasco, Emeril Lagasse kicks a pot of gumbo up a notch as the studio audience responds with a Pavlovian "Bam!" A gleeful Jacques Torres rubs his hands as if preparing to drown a baby in hollandaise sauce. Ming Tsai flourishes a pair of lobsters rampant like nunchuks, while the Iron Chefs audition for a remake of *The Seven Samurai.* Naturally, my *paisan* Mario Batali shows off his designer orange clogs. More jovial than the Man in the Moon, Mario is worth sixty-five million dollars. If he were a dietician at a Scalabrini Center, preparing strained zucchini for the decrepit and dying, he would make thirty thousand a year.

Here the ghost of Cato of Utica interrupts, or maybe the late media critic Neil Postman: "*When the Republic is imperiled, good citizenship demands serious viewing!*" True. But despite a communications degree and a stint in broadcasting, I get tubed whenever I channel-surf. CNN is too relentless, Fox too abusive, C-Span too boring, CNBC too wired. In a desert of lies and delusions, the Food Network seems a genuine oasis, even though it is actually a mirage. The same thing happened in Horace's day. Resigning from the Senate, where political debate had become a sham, a certain Catius abandoned his Stoic self-help group and enrolled in a culinary school. He was not alone. Defection had become contagious. Overnight, Rome's educated and professional classes stopped attending conferences on civics and philosophy and flocked to cooking lectures. As the empire grew, so did the influence of its celebrity chefs.

Consider Marcus Gavius Apicius, the reputed author of *De re coquinaria* (*The Art of Cooking*), who flourished in the reign of Tiberius. A gourmet and a showman, Apicius is credited with inventing various dishes and sauces in which refined delicacy was taken to sadistic extremes. According to Pliny the Elder, he fattened his pigs on currants and pine nuts, then drowned them in wine laced with cloves and cinnamon. The alleged inventor of *foie gras,* he force-fed his geese dried figs and honey to enlarge their livers. He also stuffed his guests. To titillate the jaded, Apicius served nightingale tongues as hors d'oeuvres, but hoarded the costlier and tastier flamingo tongues for himself. A jetsetter before jets, he commandeered a galleon and sailed to Libya, having heard of the boasted size and sweetness of the shrimps taken near its coast.

Disappointed by the prawns offered by the local fishermen who came alongside in their boats, Apicius ordered his crew to weigh anchor and return him to his villa at Minturnae in Campania without ever going ashore. His imperial appetite made him Caesar's rival. At the capital fish market, he once outbid Tiberius, spending five thousand sesterces for a three-pound mullet. Such profligacy inspired the future emperors Otho, Vitellius, and Heliogabulus to plunder the treasury and feast on roasted ostrich, camel heels, and stuffed sow's womb. Domitian convened a midnight session of the Senate to decide how to best cook a giant turbot he had received as a gift. The debate lasted till dawn, and the cost in candle wax could have fed the entire Subura. When the money ran out, the party ended. After squandering a hundred million sesterces and overwhelmed with debt, Apicius calculated he had only ten million left, not nearly enough to satisfy his cravings, and killed himself.

Apicius set a terrible precedent for today's super chefs. Hannelore Kohl, Bernard Loiseau, and Clemens Wilmenrod all committed suicide. Epicurus may have counseled moderation, but what good is moderation in our celebrity culture? The road to excess leads to the palace of syndication, but if economists are right, this is a good thing. Under aegis of the free market, excess is a blessing. Luxury crowns the rich, comforts the middle class, and spurs the poor. A secret alchemy transforms private vices into public goods, claim the wizards of Wall Street, so diatribes are not only misguided but pointless. That is why I confine myself to the kitchen. When my spleen throbs from the latest corporate scandal or military press conference, I mince garlic and savor the sardonic wit of Leonardo Sciascia, Sicily's greatest novelist. His taste for moral paradox is evident in this scene from *One Way or Another*.

At a religious retreat, where fasting ought to be the norm, the worldly priest Don Gaetano spreads a sumptuous table for his wealthy guests. He scorns those fools who pretend not to care what they eat, or who are so naturally uncouth and ill-bred as to be genuinely indifferent. Devoted to French cuisine, Don Gaetano eulogizes François Vatel, the legendary chef of the Prince of Condé, who stabbed himself on April 24, 1671, at a two-thousand-seat banquet honoring Louis XIV at the Château de Chantilly. Proposing a toast, Don Gaetano compares Vatel to Cato of Utica: both men of honor who fell on their swords. True, the latter killed himself because of the loss of freedom, while the former dispatched himself because a delivery of fish failed to arrive. But both acts had the same value before God, because they were motivated by the same self-respect.

The guests object. There's self-respect and self-respect. The monsignor is indulging in Sicilian sophistry. Even God Almighty can't compare fish—one of many courses for Louis the Sun King—to freedom. "And why not?" Don Gaetano retorts. "Let's leave God out of this, since we know nothing more of His opinions than what is convenient to salvation, and our desire for salvation probably prejudices our knowledge. So leaving God aside, and granting that self-respect is a valid choice, Vatel is a better example of it than Cato of Utica, for the fish ought to have arrived and in fact did arrive an hour after he had killed himself. Whereas freedom . . . ?"

Food for thought in these imperial times.

SPEAKING OF WHICH, supper is almost ready. You strike me as a *buona forchetta*, a hearty eater. Good! Prepare yourself for a full plate; in Latin, *lanx satura*. Once reserved for a sacred tray heaped with offerings for the gods, this phrase later applied to any teeming dish. As it passed from the temple to the kitchen, *satura* changed from an adjective to a noun meaning antipasto, buffet, mixed grill, stuffing, or hash. In short, a confection of disparate ingredients. Even today, Lazian cooks call a meal whipped up from leftovers and miscellaneous scraps a *Romanella*.

This ancient culinary term is also the root word for satire, that most Roman of literary genres. "*Satura quidem tota nostra est*," Quintilian said. "Satire is wholly ours." A farrago, medley, hodgepodge, or mélange, its social criticism shoots from the gut and leaps for the throat. Given its kitchen origins, satire often explores the cultural significance of food and wrestles with the

ethical dimensions of cooking; hence the importance of gastron-
omy and gastroenterology in Roman literature. When Horace
mocks pretentious dinners, or Petronius cringes at vulgar catering, or Juvenal gripes about stingy hosts, they place civilization on
the cutting board. The proud owner of a complete set of kitchen
knives, I follow their example.

Bitter Greens satirizes modern food production and packaging
but draws its themes, techniques, and imagery from the classical
kitchen. The best place to chew on history, politics, and economics is not the groves of the academy but the aisles of the supermarket. Consider this book a symposium, then, a banquet with
intellectual discussion. Beginning with a keynote and ending with
an after-dinner speech, it offers six thought-provoking dishes.
Nothing *too* fancy, mind. Only the French eat brains. As the first-
century bon vivant Aulus Gellius stipulates: "A good table should
aim not so much at extravagance as an absence of meanness. Likewise, dinner conversation should not deal with tiresome or complicated matters but be intriguing and agreeable, calculated to
improve our minds and cheer our spirits. This end can be
attained only if topics are confined to matters of everyday life,
such as we have no time to consider in the press of public affairs."
For the time-starved citizens of a fast-food nation, where public
discourse is unpalatable and dyspepsia is the hallmark of power,
the safest topic is food.

This collection's core is organized like the six parts of a
Southern Italian meal (*antipasto, primo, secondo, contorno, dolce,* and
caffè). Since our talk will include the fall of republics, the ruins of
history, and the twilight of ethnicity, I have prepared a meal best
served in November, the month of the dead, when places are set
for deceased relatives and care packages are left in cemeteries,
usually scavenged by the homeless. For the poor of the Mezzogiorno, food and death are closely connected. "Even in heaven,"
one proverb states, "meals must be stretched." Thrift, thrift, Horatio. The funeral baked meats did coldly furnish forth the marriage
tables.

Opposite is a formal menu, prepared by your host. Each
course corresponds to an essay, and during dinner, I will share the
actual recipe.

MENU

Antipasto
Abruzzese Soppressata, Mozzarella, and Olives

Primo
Calabrian Onion Soup

Secondo
Tripe alla Romana

Contorno
Apulian Broccoli Rabe Salad

Dolce
Sicilian Chocolate Cake

Caffè
Neapolitan Espresso

But before we dig in, some toasts are in order:

Five wonderful books provided background material for this collection: John Dickey's *Delizia: The Epic History of Italians and their Food* (NY: Free Press, 2008); David Downie's *Cooking the Roman Way: Authentic Recipes from the Home Cooks and Trattorias of Rome* (HarperCollins, 2002); Patrick Faas's *Around the Roman Table: Food and Feasting in Ancient Rome* (Palgrave Macmillan, 2003); Ilaria Giacosa's *A Taste of Ancient Rome* (University of Chicago Press, 1992); and Mary Taylor Simeti's *Pomp and Sustenance: Twenty-Five Centuries of Sicilian Food* (Knopf, 1989). The recipes and memories, however, come from my parents, grandparents, aunts, uncles, and cousins. Thank you, *carissimi*, for feeding me body and soul.

Others also have nourished me: fellow foody Catherine Rankovic, without whose faith and support this book would not have been written; agent Sara Crowe, who coached me through sixty rejection letters; SUNY stalwarts Elise Brauckmann, Cathleen Collins, Gary Dunham, Dana Foote, Fran Keneston, Amanda Lanne, and James Peltz, who brought this manuscript to press;

administrators Peter Bardaglio, Howard Erlich, Leslie Lewis, Jim Malek, Marian Mesrobian MacCurdy, Diane McPherson, Sally Parr, Thomas Rochon, Kathleen Roundtree, and Peggy Williams, who granted me sabbaticals and reassigned time to complete this project; colleagues Barbara Adams, Susan Adams, Rick and Geri Anderson, Ingrid Arnesen, Bonnie Auslander, Anita Belil, Lin Betancourt, Miriam Brody, Tom Brooks, Cory Brown, Louise Cannon, Jamie Caracciolo, Cathleen Chaffee, Paul Cody, Christine Coleman, Stephen Cope, Annette Corth, Robert Danberg, Ron Denson, Sandra Dutkowsky, Rhian Ellis, Elaine Farrugia, Meg Favreau, David Flanagan, Peter Fortunato, Victoria Fullard, Cheryl Kutcher Gatling, Maggie Gerrity, Linda Godfrey, Andrei Guruianu, Trena Haffenden, Paul and Kristen Hamill, Ricardo Hasse, Roger Hecht, Liz Holmes, Eric Machan Howd, Edward Hower, Lynn Hyde, Sarah Jefferis, Tom Kerr, Bob Klier, Marlene Kobre, Nick Kowalczyk, Ron Lancia, Joni Landau, Elizabeth Lawson, Annette Levine, Katharyn Howd Machan, Jeanne Mackin, Sabatino Maglione, Caroline Manring, Joan Marcus, Gigi Marks, Katie Marks, Bridget Meeds, Ginny Miller, Angelina Mirabella, Jerry Mirskin, Seph Murtagh, Kim Nesta, Jason Ockert, Mary Beth O'Connor, Shona Ramaya, Mary Ann Rishel, Valorie Rockney, Rosie Parsons, Cathy Penner, Lucia Perillo, Steve Poleskie, Eileen Schell, Patricia Spencer, Scott and Nancy Smith, Maura Stephens, Elizabeth Silaj Teskey, Bob Sullivan, Kate Sullivan, James Stafford, Jennifer Strickland, Catherine Taylor, Maria Vargas, Gladys Varona-Lacey, Jack Wang, Jaime Warburton, Rachel Wenrick, Fred Wilcox, and Ellen Zaslaw, who provided a decade of feedback and encouragement; and above all, my wife, Sharon Elizabeth Ahlers, with whom I've shared fifteen thousand meals over the past twenty years. She gives life savor.

And now, *cenemus!*

KEYNOTE

Lucullan Feasts

LUCULLAN FEASTS

WEGMANS FOOD MARKETS, INC., Central New York's leading supermarket chain, once honored me with a Roman banquet. I still don't know whether this boon was random or deliberate, whether fortune or demographics had smiled on me. But on the eve of Columbus Day, 1999, a package arrived at my home containing a videotape and an autopen letter from President Danny Wegman stamped with the company logo. "Dr. Di Renzo," the letter announced, "WEGMANS INVITES YOU TO SAVOR A TRUE TASTE OF SICILY!"

The accompanying tape was a dub of a television special broadcast in March promoting Wegmans' Italian Classics line, a staple in my kitchen ever since I moved to Ithaca and left behind the ethnic groceries of Syracuse's Little Italy. Led by Nella Neeck, a "recipe-development specialist," a company team had journeyed to Sicily to research its culture and cuisine. Traveling through Palermo, Agrigento, Catania, and Trapani, Wegmans' scouts had located many folk dishes. Noted chef Marchesa Anna Tasca Lanza, the flyer promised, would teach soccer moms how to prepare *involtini di melanzane con capellini*, fried eggplant rolls stuffed with angel hair.

Curious, I popped the tape into the VCR. An Italianate woman with a soup-bowl haircut stood on a hill overlooking Agrigento's Valle dei Templi. Her Eddie Bauer wardrobe transformed the Greek ruins into a picnic ground. "Greetings from the sunny Mediterranean!" she hailed. ("*Salve!*" I returned.) "Join us as we explore Wegmans' latest discovery in our search to bring your family the great tastes of Italy. I'm Nella Neeck, and welcome to Sicily! Stay tuned as we explore this magical Mediterranean isle and learn to cook an easy and authentic Sicilian meal."

Easy *and* authentic? Lady, nothing authentic is easy. My Sicilian Nonna spent weeks preparing Seven Sacrament Salad, an elaborate seafood marinade served on Christmas Eve. Now she is

3

dead, and so are the relatives for whom she cooked. Their voices haunted the soundtrack as a synthesized chorus of ancestral ghosts hummed an ancient hymn, the same ethnic wailing heard in *Gladiator* and other swords-and-sandals epics. As the wordless chant continued, Sicilian landmarks appeared in a series of dissolves: the fluted colonnade of the Temple of Hera; a flowering almond orchard in Piana degli Albanesi; the Arab domes of San Giovanni degli Eremiti; the neoclassical façade of the Teatro Massimo Opera House, the frieze from Palermo's Triumphal Arch; the Norman Cathedral of Monreale. Beneath these time-stained monuments scrolled titles in decorative script: "*History . . . tradition . . . authenticity . . . passion!*"

Familiar sights. As a toddler, I had spent a year in Sicily recovering from a near-fatal case of dysentery contracted during a family vacation in Abruzzo. The doctors had recommended sea air and a citrus diet, so my mother spirited me to her hometown of Villabate, a suburb of Palermo, where a prolonged convalescence formed a treasure chest of memories. I could have sworn Wegmans used these fragments of time to create this kaleidoscope of images. Terra-cotta roof tiles baked in the sun, rake-armed field hands harvested ripened olives, wheels of Peccorino Romano cured *al fresco,* painted donkey carts displayed scenes from *The Song of Roland,* colorful fishing boats bobbed in the harbor at Mondello, and shoppers haggled in the Vuccciria Market.

I shook my head. Publicists had turned Persephone's Island into an infomercial. Well, worse things have happened over the past twenty-five centuries. Verres, the Roman governor whom Cicero prosecuted for graft and extortion, plundered Sicily's temples for his private art collection. At least this promotional video helped local business and boosted *agriturismo.*

"Sicily's tragic past has shaped its unique cuisine," Nella explained. "The list of those who have invaded and conquered this island is a long one, from Phoenicians and Greeks to Romans and Spaniards. No wonder a tourism slogan says, 'INVADE SICILY: EVERYONE ELSE HAS!'" These invaders brought their own gods and their own food, as every Sicilian pantry testifies: raisins, introduced by Arabs; tomatoes, brought by Spaniards; olives from ancient Greeks."

A kinder, gentler conqueror, Wegmans held contests, not hostages. Obeying instructions, I returned the circular to my neighborhood store, where I received a sixteen-ounce bottle of extra-virgin olive oil and was entered in a raffle for a gourmet dinner to be held at the store's Culinary School of the Arts on Friday, November 19. Five weeks later, an answering-machine message informed me I had won. The store manager and his wife were eager to meet me. Would I RSVP the executive chef? I was entitled to bring five guests.

Flabbergasted, I nursed mixed feelings about claiming my prize. On the one hand, this banquet was the perfect opportunity to celebrate the move to Ithaca, repay colleagues for their support, and socialize outside the bell jar of the academy. The store manager chaired the board of trustees for the Tompkins County Library, while his wife organized the altar linens and managed the gift shop at Immaculate Conception Church. They would make fine neighbors.

On the other hand, I remained shaken by Wegmans' conquest of Sicily and its laser-like targeting. How did Wegmans get my new address? I had settled here only four months ago. A recently tenured professor of classical rhetoric, I fit the chain's customer profile (a white-collar professional earning $30,000 to $60,000), but how did Wegmans *know* I was a professor? The circular had addressed me as doctor, though I had never provided this information when applying for my Syracuse shopper's card. And what was I doing with a shopper's card, anyway, pawning personal data to slick marketers? Had my buying habits determined the outcome of the contest? An Old World man in a New Age town, I splurge every week on Italian groceries, each canned artichoke, loaf of artisan bread, and jar of Nutella recorded by the supermarket computer. This self-indulgence dictated stocking patterns that disadvantaged working-class shoppers. Feeling trapped and guilty, I recalled how Cicero had faced a similar dilemma in etiquette.

In December, 44 B.C., Cicero was wintering at Puteoli when he received a message from Julius Caesar asking if he could come to dinner. After the civil war, Caesar had spared Cicero, so a *quid pro quo* was expected; but Caesar's casual request was a veiled command to billet two thousand troops. Should Cicero resist? With Caesar a week's march away, he wrote Atticus, who reminded Cicero that the laws of hospitality trump politics. Besides, when one is defeated and compromised, dining with Caesar beats dying with Cato. Wise words. My Catholic Worker days are far behind me, and despite qualms, I prefer shopping at Wegmans rather than the Greenstar Food Co-op. Since it would be hypocritical and ungrateful to refuse, I confirmed my attendance and invited my wife and two other couples, all local writers and artists.

"This should be a Lucullan feast," I promised.

WEGMANS DID NOT PROVIDE a *triclinium*, three couches arranged in a horseshoe around a serving table, but a teeming banquet awaited us upstairs, cordoned off from the milling shoppers, who had caught a whiff of celebrity. Our dinner party consisted of nine people, following the guidelines of Cicero's contemporary Varro: *No fewer than the Graces, no more than the Muses.* The chef, stolen from Robert Congel, CEO of the Pyramid Companies and father of the Carousel Mall, seated me at the head of the table and practically crowned me with bay. Solemn as Buster Keaton, he deflected all compliments and concentrated on serving. The more convivial manager patted my shoulder, poured the Chianti, and promoted the store with each course.

The stuffed jumbo prawns were packed in ice and trucked this morning from Boston, where field buyers˙communicate via short-wave and cellular phone to offshore fishermen, who use sonar and computers to secure the best catches. The romaine in the Caesar's salad came from Cornell's hydroponics greenhouse with whirring twenty-foot fans, while the olives were imported from Sicily in brine-filled oak casks. As for the filet mignon, so rare and succulent that it bled like a martyr in the arena, it was handpicked from a herd of Texas longhorns, just for this occasion. Wegmans, he bragged, does everything possible to treat its customers like kings.

Or Roman emperors, I almost said, but I promised my wife to behave. Still—as the congratulations flowed with the wine, as our hosts toasted one-stop shopping, centralized inventory, and the wonders of globalization—I wondered if every customer is a potential Nero, and remembered an incident I had witnessed three years ago at the DeWitt Wegmans.

I was pricing shrimp in the Fisherman's Wharf when two burly stockers dumped a basket of crabs on the display table. Hundreds struggled in the crushed ice, a failed rebellion. Resembling *mirmillones*, gladiators with fish-shaped helmets, the crabs brandished their claws. *Morituri te salutamus!* We who are about to die salute you! A melee erupted. The wounded flipped on their backs, while the determined frothed at the mouth. They were beautiful and splendidly cruel: their pincers tipped a reddish orange, their plates and leggings dabbed with blue. One champion stood out, an indomitable runt with a chipped claw whom I nicknamed Spartacus. He dispatched an opponent with a single thrust to the underbelly and used its corpse to shield himself from attackers. Around the miniature arena, customers cheered and bet. Flourishing his claws like castanets, Spartacus danced a fandango on the bodies of the dead, until a Syracuse Orange fan snatched him for a tailgate party at the Carrier Dome.

This memory prompted me to speak. Tactfully, since I dislike biting the hand that feeds me, I asked whether convenience and selection might cost too much. As a veteran shopper and occasional gardener, I marvel at Wegmans' produce section, mountains of fresh vegetables and fruits always miraculously in season; but such produce is picked by migrants and grown by failing upstate farmers, like those die-hard Sicilians struggling to raise onions in the Canastota mucklands. When harvests are bad, they work for minimum wage at the Utica Wegmans.

This ambivalence extends to decor, I continued. I treasure Wegmans' Old World atmosphere. After the standardized Shop Rites of suburban New Jersey, how wonderful to shop in a European open-air market! The chain's flagship store even boasts a section of imported Italian kitchenware. When I first saw those Ballarini skillets and Bormioli coffee cups, I nearly swooned, for Wegmans had replicated the miracle of Loretto. Spoon by spoon, saucer by saucer, the company had transported my cousin Fiorina's kitchen from Vasto, a seaside resort in Abruzzo, to Pittsford, New York. But displaced peasants make these products in the sweatshops squeezed between the Adriatic and the Majella Mountains.

And so, I confessed, I remain torn. I am grateful for Wegmans' generous selection of ethnic specialties—for bitter greens like dandelions, cardoons, and broccoli rabe; for imported cold cuts like Bolognese *mortadella* and Abruzzese *soppressata*; for affordable arborio rice and espresso coffee beans; for fresh baked Italian bread and decent homemade *cannoli*. But I regret, no, resent, how Wegmans crushes hundreds of Italian greengrocers, butchers, and dairy farmers in Albany, Utica, Syracuse, Rochester, and Buffalo, then hires them as underpaid consultants, buyers, and assistant section managers, just as Rome subjugated provincials and barbarians before offering them citizenship.

Growing up in Rochester's Ukrainian neighborhood and troubled by the Kodak layoffs, the manager sympathized. Today, the little guy can't make it, unless the big guy helps. But Wegmans is no Wal-Mart. Among *Fortune*'s Top Hundred Companies to Work for in America, the chain is devoted to its employees and committed to the regional economy. Take DiBella's, Rochester's most popular Italian deli. Last year, Danny Wegman noticed the long lines outside the North Union Street store near corporate headquarters. Impressed, he asked Joey DiBella to help Wegmans create a sub shop in its supermarkets. During negotiations, Danny learned that back in 1918 Joey's great-grandfather ran a grocery near where Danny's grandfather had begun *his* grocery two years earlier. Eight decades later, the two family businesses had reunited to bring back "old-fashioned goodness"—an authentic Italian sub made on a freshly baked roll!

Good copy, I conceded. This anecdote, in fact, appears on the sandwich bags for Wegmans Old Fashioned Submarines, illustrated with a picture of the luncheon counter of Wegmans' original Clinton Avenue Store, circa 1930. As I learned on Madison Avenue, sepia sells. But neither the factory workers in denim overhauls nor the sales clerks in straw hats could eat in DiBella's now. The family business, I pointed out, has become a national franchise. Gravitating towards the suburbs of such Rust Belt towns as Ann Arbor, Buffalo, and Cleveland, DiBella's caters to white-collar professionals, who prefer their nostalgia spic-and-span and dislike riff-raff interrupting their power lunches. Given these demographic strictures, DiBella's can't afford to serve mechanics with dirty fingernails or locate in crumbling ethnic neighborhood.

Blue-collar dagos are off the radar. They and the mom-and-pop stores they ran or patronized have vanished, just as the Coca-Cola bottling plant swallowed Mount Allegro, Rochester's Little Italy. If you can cut a deal with corporate America, you have a shot. If not, fugheddaboudit.

AT THIS POINT, my guests chimed in. Law is a tangle, medicine a mystery, but everyone feels qualified to discuss economics over tiramisu. Wasn't my diatribe one-sided? The end of the Cold War surely had taught us the merits of capitalism. Ten years ago, as demonstrators dismantled the Berlin Wall, Coca-Cola reps passed free samples through the holes. Only Marxist professors objected. Could I deny that the past decade had been one of unparalleled prosperity? The NASDAQ had shot through the stratosphere, high-school dropouts had jump-started dotcoms, and the fed had paid off a $290 billion deficit. (This was, of course, 1999—before the dot.com bust, 9/11, and the near meltdown of the world's financial system in late 2008.) Since click-and-order had replaced brick-and-mortar, hillbillies could install satellite dishes on tarpaper shacks and graying hippies in remote ecovillages could drive hybrids. Yes, someone should address the widening income gap and police Third-World sweatshops; but for all its disruptions, globalization raised the world's standard of living by lowering prices and increasing the variety of staples. Adam Smith was right: "It is not from the benevolence of the butcher, the brewer, or the baker that we expect our dinner, but from their regard to their own interest."

The manager agreed, but a supermarket's interest must be its customers' interest. For the past eighty years, Wegmans has anticipated consumer trends. During the Depression, brothers Walt and Jack Wegman installed a three-hundred-seat cafeteria, refrigerated meat displays, and a state-of-the-art produce section with vaporized water sprays. After the war, Walter's son Bob pioneered frozen TV dinners, self-service shopping, and computerized checkout lines. His son Danny, a Harvard MBA who had returned to Rochester to apprentice as a butcher, faces the challenge of globalization. In this brave new economy, regional supermarket chains compete with national bulk warehouses and urban food importers. To stay in the game, Wegmans must slash prices and

democratize gourmet specialties. So far, expansion and diversification have paid off. With fifty-one megastores in Central New York
alone, and twenty more satellites in New Jersey, Pennsylvania, Virginia, and Maryland, Wegmans earns $3.8 billion annually. It
remains Upstate New York's most thriving company because it
thinks globally but sells locally.

Consider Wegmans' Italian Classics line. Wherever the company travels in Sicily, Tuscany, or Campania, it plants suppliers
and harvests canned goods. Wegmans found a partner in Naples
who mills his own flour, using a blend of Italian and North American hard durum wheat semolina and pure mountain water. That's
why Wegmans pasta is so hearty! The global village turns provincial grocers into cosmopolitans. Clerking in the Rochester Wegmans back in the Sixties, the manager never dreamed of
becoming an expert on extra-virgin olive oil. Did the professor
know Wegmans offers three different brands from three different
regions with varying soil types and altitudes? Terrain makes a difference. Olives pressed from trees in hillier land taste bolder, for
example. Wegmans blends two or three different strains to produce a unique profile.

The manager cell-phoned for samples. Campania, he
explained, was smooth and faintly herbal: great for pasta and
tomatoes. Puglia's sharper, tangier flavor paired well with seafood
and meat; while Tuscany's fruitier flavor and peppery finish were
perfect for salads. No Sicilian oil yet, he apologized, but Wegmans
was developing one. Something light and buttery for breads. The
guy was as eloquent on the subject as Cicero. But true believers
always become rhapsodic when singing the praises of globalization. Once, the chair of the economics department, a slight old
man with a stiff comb-over but a heart of gold, faculty advisor for
the Ithaca College Republicans, director of the Southern Tier
Center for Economic Development, and recipient of the Wal-Mart
Chair in Economics, launched into an encomium in the Wegmans
produce section.

"Antonio," he declared, with a sweep of his bony arm, "this is
the loaves and the fishes!" Never before, he maintained, has the
world seen such abundance; and what generates this bursting
piñata, this cornucopia, this all-you-can-eat buffet? The engine of
free trade! Like a catalytic converter, capitalism transforms fava

beans into Walkmen, portabellas into floppy disks, without central planning or government coercion. How did the planet know Antonio wanted to cook *perciatelli* with shrimp and fennel today? What telepathy enabled Italian flour mills, Japanese fishing fleets, and California farms to coordinate and deliver these ingredients at an affordable price? This works the same in every country, rich or poor.

"Marx was wrong!" he crowed, jabbing my chest. Capitalism has not impoverished the masses. If anything, capitalism has poured a horn of plenty upon the masses, who frequently tried to sabotage the adoption of life-saving innovations. But legislative reforms and union pressure never improved the human condition: capitalism did because it put consumers, not workers, first. "That's something you hidebound European socialists can't accept! Consumers are sovereign; their wishes shape the world!"

I held my tongue. Never blaspheme in church, even if you're an atheist. Besides, Wegmans each year donates 6,000 tons of food, 350 tractor trailers' worth, to food banks and street pantries in the Dioceses of Rochester and Syracuse. If capitalism fed the hungry, how could I, a former soup-kitchen volunteer, criticize the corporal works of mercy? Maybe I was blind to the wonders of the market. All the same, as I hunted for a good cabbage, I recalled this wasn't the first time a global market had poured abundance on sovereign consumers. According to Livy, civilization began when a she-wolf suckled two abandoned babes. Ever since, we have paid dearly for the she-wolf's milk.

CLASSICAL ROME DEVELOPED the West's first market economy. Without a sophisticated network of estate farms, domestic and foreign ports, and profitable colonies, the city would have starved. During the Late Republic and Early Empire, Rome's population was a million inhabitants. Impressive by ancient standards, but not nearly as many customers as Wegmans serves in a week. Nevertheless, the city needed extensive supplies—twenty to forty million *modii* of grain a year, about 150–300,000 tons, plus extensive supplies of oil and wine. Naturally, it was far cheaper to ship food across the Mediterranean than over land. Rome imported grain from Sardinia, Sicily, and Egypt, oil from Spain and Africa, spices and dried fruits from the Middle East and India.

Contemporary pundits tout the global economy's spontaneous order, but Rome's enormous conglomeration of interdependent markets was not spontaneous. Then as now, military force created lines of transportation and communication and determined trade patterns. Feeding the economy, militarism inspired mass grocery sprees, and Roman triumphs functioned like the Macy's parade. "On such days," reports historian Florence Dupont, "there was too much of everything. The waste was willful and wanton: when people could gorge themselves no more, whole sides of beef as yet untouched would be heaved into the Tiber." Such potlatch was sacred. The entire populace delighted in the favor of the gods and the opulence flowing from the wealth of the nobility and the spoils of war. Indeed, the fecundity of the nobles' livestock and their good fortune on the battlefield bore the same name, *felicitas*. At public feasts, the poor staggered under delicacies, experiencing divine bounty at first hand in the streets of their own city. Public extravagance proved that private austerity was not a matter of shortages or necessity but a form of patriotism.

Not every day could be Mardi Gras, of course. That would lead to *luxuria,* wasteful idleness. Citizens who dishonored themselves in this way were condemned by the censors, driven from their order, and heaped with public shame. Such offenders had been destroyed by their *gulla* their gullet. But those moralizing Romans had placed themselves in a double bind. Elites were expected and encouraged to indulge in conspicuous consumption. Ostentation trumpeted reputation, attracted political patronage, and justified the Roman way of life. Spendthrifts were lionized because they provided vicarious thrills for the masses. Julius Caesar conquered as much through superior credit as superior arms. When Caesar pursued Pompey to Egypt, he arrived in Alexandria on market day. Merchant stalls and customers packed the docks. The boy pharaoh Ptolemy and his advisors expected Caesar to force his way through the emporium, upsetting the populace and giving the Egyptians a propaganda advantage; instead, Caesar and his troops shopped their way through and captured the palace. That is the pattern of empire. Whether it conquers through violence, diplomacy, or trade, conquest is conquest and always manures corruption.

Nothing could stop the spread of *luxuria,* particularly when it came to eating. Tabletops became prestigious objects, made from such valuable woods as walnut, lemon, maple, cypress, oak, and beech. Some male patricians spent so much on expensive tables that their enthusiasm rivaled their wives' fetish for jewels. Cicero's banquet table cost as much as his villa at Puteoli. Upper-class families squandered such huge sums on food that the Senate feared capital erosion. Accordingly, Cato the Elder and other hardliners instituted sumptuary laws. They prohibited such delicacies as fatted chickens and pan-fried dormice and restricted the number of guests. During the Roman games, dinner hosts took a public oath not to spend more than twenty-five *sesterces* per dinner, except on vegetables, bread, and wine. Foreign wines were forbidden, and no more than one hundred pounds of silver could be used at table. When public outrage became unbearable, the Senate passed more stringent laws but to no avail. Some patricians resorted to smuggling. Others accepted wild game from tenants and bought dolphin and swordfish from former slaves for three pennies a pound.

But the most defiant epicure was Lucius Licinius Lucullus, whose name has become synonymous with lavish dining. Once a noted general, Lucullus had commanded the Third Mithridatic War, until a smoking-room deal wrecked his career. At Cicero's suggestion, the Senate demoted Lucullus and gave his commission to Pompey the Great, whom Lucullus called "a vulture scavenging on the scraps of other men's victories." Disillusioned and disgusted, Lucullus withdrew from public life and became notorious for extravagance. Using the vast treasure he had amassed in the Near East, he constructed splendid gardens outside of Rome on the Pincian Hill, the future haunt of the nymphomaniac empress Messalina, as well as splendid villas around Tusculum and Neapolis. Located on an island off a promontory of the Bay of Naples, Lucullus's villa out-did San Simeon. Engineers had suspended hills over vast tunnels and girdled the estate residences with sea channels and artificial streams for the breeding of fish. His colossal hatcheries and aquariums dwarfed the famous eel ponds of his cousin and fellow general Lucius Licinius Murena.

Moralists called Lucullus "Xerxes in a toga," but the smart set clamored to dine with him. He sorted the banqueters into different rooms, rather like the various restaurants in an old-fashioned German railroad station. In the Apollo Room, reserved for his most intimate or prestigious guests, Lucullus spent a thousand *sesterces* a head. Slaves laid precious foods upon tables of ivory, silver, or carved tortoise shell. Other guests settled for goblets of inlaid gold, but diners in the Apollo Room drank from great hollowed gems. After a recital accompanied by thirty hors d'oeuvres, Lucullus gave these VIPs the privilege of watching their next course die. Mullets bred in mountain lakes and transplanted to his estates, or trout brought live from a particular stream in Etruria, expired slowly in exquisite glass jars placed before the diners. Guests judged each death throe. The fish that leapt highest and longest supposedly tasted the best. If that seems cruel, observe how Wegmans shoppers, especially double-chinned matrons, tap on the lobster tank and wait for a reaction. They always choose the most riled lobster.

Consumed by spite and self-contempt, Lucullus lived on the outskirts of Roman society. More often than not he ate alone, but pretended not to care. Once, when a modest repast had been prepared, he flew into a rage and summoned the chef and steward. The servants apologized but, since there were no guests, they had assumed the master wanted nothing costly. Lucullus laughed. "What?" he sneered. "Didn't you know that today Lucullus dines with Lucullus?" Even so, traces of decency remained in his character. He donated his delectable gardens to the city, built Rome's first public library, subsidized schools of philosophy, and studied horticulture. He introduced the sweet cherry and the apricot to Italy and developed the strain of Swiss chard bearing his name.

But for the most part, he remained aloof. Rome had broken his heart, and he could not forgive it. Sensing his pain and isolation, Cicero and Pompey arranged a rapprochement. Spotting Lucullus in the forum, they asked him to consider a petition. Gladly, Lucullus said. What was it? "We desire," said Cicero, "to dine with you today just as you would have dined by yourself." Overcome, Lucullus sobbed and covered his face, and Cicero hugged him. From that day, the three men supped regularly, despite irreconcilable differences. The best perk of civilization.

THE WEGMANS BANQUET lasted three hours. Wine and conversation had mellowed me. Ten years ago, I confessed, I might have stormed out at several points in our debate. Possibly, I would have rejected the invitation outright and published a letter in an alternative newspaper. But I was glad I had come, and my conscience barely smarted. Only yesterday, I had taught *Pro Murena*, Cicero's witty defense of political expediency and the polite lie. After foiling the Catalinarian conspiracy, Cicero found himself embroiled in a campaign scandal. His co-consul, General Murena, more slithery than his prized eels, had accepted bribes, but was that fact worth invalidating Rome's first election after a failed coup? Concrete order was needed, not abstract principle. After all, we lived in Romulus's shit hole, not Plato's Republic. The Senate convulsed with laughter, even that sourpuss Cato the Younger, who had called for Murena's impeachment. A vain, garrulous wise guy, Cicero could forgive much for a good joke and a good meal. And I told the story of how this ardent Republican once hosted Julius Caesar at his winter home.

Caesar arrived in Puteoli on the second night of the Saturnalia. Cicero's villa already was so crammed with soldiers that no dining room remained for the guest of honor. Caesar apologized for the inconvenience and retired to the guest house, where he intended to rest and review the army accounts. Cicero had twenty-four hours to prepare dinner, but martial law cramped the festivities. A camp had been pitched on the front lawn, and the villa was in a state of defense. Nevertheless, Cicero put the soldiers to good use. Grunts helped the scullions peel turnips, while centurions built and operated spitted barbecues. On the menu was whole roasted pig, introduced in Cicero's consulship by Publius Servilius Rullus. The chef ordered forty boars butchered.

At one o'clock the following afternoon, Caesar finished business with his finance secretary and chief engineer Lucius Cornelius Balbus. He strolled on the beach until two and then went to the bath for a massage. At three, he arrived at the villa, anointed and dressed in Tyrrhenian purple. Cicero remained warily polite, until Caesar embraced him. "At last!" he said. "Ever since you persuaded the Senate to make Balbus here a citizen, I've longed to dine with you!" When required, Caesar could be warm and gracious. Cicero reciprocated by seating him at the couch of honor.

Everyone observed the two men. Physically, host and guest were opposites: Cicero, plump and jovial; Caesar, gaunt and sardonic. Intellectually, they were alike. Scrupulously avoiding politics, their conversation stuck to literature. Although Caesar's regimen of emetics allowed him to eat and drink heartily, he seemed frail and vulnerable. Epilepsy, Cicero thought. Since Caesar had become dictator, the attacks had become more frequent. Poor man. Blame the vintage Falernian, but Cicero felt tender towards his foe. Even Caesar's habit of tracing his bald spot with an index finger seemed endearing rather than maddening. When Caesar became pale and woozy, Cicero escorted him to the vomitorium and never apologized for his solicitude.

"*For that evening,*" he wrote Atticus, "*we were human beings together.*"

Touched by this story, the manager's wife quoted Psalm 133: "How precious it is when brothers dwell together in unity." Yes, I said, that's Christian *caritas.* But it's almost as precious when enemies eat together without unity. That's Roman *civitas,* and usually it's the best we can do. Whether this is a miracle of compromise or a compromised miracle, I could not say; but it sure beat the alternative. For that reason, the manager interjected, he supported globalization. Nations don't have to like each other to do business, but more trade means less war. We convert enemies to our way of life without necessarily converting them to our point of view. Why else, he asked, slapping my back, would a Sicilian marchesa sell family recipes to an American supermarket.

"Perhaps you're right," I demurred. Dinner was breaking up, so a rebuttal would have been inappropriate. But when I returned home, I replayed the Wegmans video.

THE COMPANY FILM CREW has transformed the Regaleali estate's ancestral kitchen into a set for the Food Network. Behind a hand-carved table stand host Nella Neeck and Marchesa Anna Tasca Lanza di Mazzarino. Nella, a culinary educator and charter member of the Produce for Better Health Foundation, believes in the ADA's National Strive for Five Program. The Marchesa, the curator of a tragic culture and a supplicant from an almost extinct class, believes in the Three Fates. Even so, the two women pretend to be sisters and imitate each other. Usually fresh-scrubbed and perky as a homecoming queen, Nella seems more mature and dignified. She wears tasteful woolens, to fight the chill from the ancient stone walls, and occasionally speaks Sicilian. The leathered and reserved Marchesa, despite a silver Pompadour and a triangular pin, acts more relaxed and American. Over gold-rimmed glasses, she looks down her beaky nose and smiles at Nella, whose affection and respect do not seem scripted.

But the cameras roll, and Nella must perform. Blinded by klieg lights and distracted by cue cards, she commits one gaffe after another. She never addresses the Marchesa by title, a terrible impertinence in Sicily. Worse, she prompts the Marchesa to promote her estate's commercial tomato sauce, even when the Marchesa indicates she would prefer not to. The hard sell smacks of *protagonismo*, self-promotion—another Sicilian taboo. Despite an occasional grimace, however, the Marchesa remains gracious. Nella comes from a land of fast foods and ATMs. To act like a Sicilian, Nella would need to suffer like a Sicilian, to live in a world of graft, car bombs, water rations, and earthquakes. Does Nella deserve that? Absolutely not. But irony finally tempers indulgence when Nella asks why the Marchesa salts her eggplants before frying. The old woman replies with a meaningful grin: "It kills the bitterness."

Spoken like a philosopher, but what else can she do? The Neecks have inherited the earth, even in Sicily. Since the 1948 ban on new noble titles, the Rotary Club Palermo Nord (Distretto 2100) removes the region's moth-eaten aristocrats from storage only for an occasional ribbon cutting or wine tasting. As a modestly successful cookbook author, Donna Anna has surrendered to the New World Order without completely hocking her dignity.

Others struggle to follow her example in a cruel global economy. Few prospects exist for classics professors, soup-kitchen directors, farmers, machinists, poets, artists, and saints. Good losers are rare, and the Roman banquet of globalization is often unpalatable. Too many people must swallow their pride, grief, and rage. Not everyone can stomach that. As the tidal gorge rises, protesters picket a McDonald's in Kabul, rioters stone a Kentucky Fried Chicken sign in Rawalpindi, and Jihadists torch a Pepsi machine in Tehran. Unless such hatred and resentment are contained, civilization—like a buffet canopy at a rowdy Palatine mixer—will collapse in a heap.

Because economic winners are rarely kind, economic losers pay the price of forbearance. Since the market showers us with benefits we do not deserve in any moral sense, it obliges us to accept equally undeserved losses of income and dignity with good grace. Economics, after all, is the science of allocating scarce resources. That may explain why human decency so often requires Hamburger Helper. Despite fleeting moments of tragic insight and heroic greatness, we are petty, vicious creatures, deluded by vanity and driven by self-interest. But if that's particularly true of us moderns, the ancients weren't paragons either. Great-hearted Cicero, who dined with his enemies, could be a shit.

After Caesar left the villa, Cicero reverted to his usual snide self. "Not the sort of guest to whom one says, 'Do stop by again!'" he wrote Atticus. "Once is enough!" On the Ides of March, when Caesar was carved like a dish for the gods, Cicero gloated: "If I had been invited to that banquet of liberty, there would have been no leftovers!" He meant Mark Antony, whose drunkenness and gluttony Cicero mocked in the Senate. But Antony, who once treated a town of thirty-five thousand to his chef's rare paste of flamingo brains, also had a taste for blood. During the proscriptions, he ordered Cicero's execution and, at the victory banquet, passed around his head and hands as party favors.

"So you see," I told the Wegmans manager, "neither classicism nor capitalism works."

We greet each other warmly whenever we meet in the supermarket. He always smiles and invites me to company events; I always bow and make excuses. As Voltaire told the Marquis De Sade, when declining a second invitation to a catered orgy: "Once is philosophy, twice is perversity."

ANTIPASTO

*Abruzzese
Soppressata,
Mozzarella,
and Olives*

*Exiles from
Cockaigne*

ABRUZZESE
SOPPRESSATA,
MOZZARELLA,
AND OLIVES

ANTIPASTO LITERALLY MEANS "before the meal." Accompanied by a glass of wine, these cold dishes welcome guests, stimulate the appetite, and ease conversation. Although some *antipasti* are as elaborate as French hors d'oeuvres and Spanish tapas, this traditional recipe is refreshingly simple.

Simplicity, however, requires quality. Use only the freshest *mozzarella* and, if possible, artisan *soppressata*. Commercial salami is riskier. Bismarck's grim joke about sausages and democracy remains all too valid. The U.S. Department of Agriculture forbids the import of Italian *soppressata*, but the best domestic brand is Columbus. The company's Farm to Fork program guarantees freshness.

INGREDIENTS
- 1 pound Abruzzese *soppressata*, sliced into ¼ inch-thick coins
- 1 pound fresh *mozzarella* medallions
- 1 pound Sicilian green olives (stuffed with garlic)

DIRECTIONS
1. Divide a large serving tray, like Gaul, into three sections.
2. Fill each section with *soppressata*, *mozzarella*, and olives, forming the Italian flag.
3. Salute and sing *Mameli's Hymn* or a rabble-rousing chorus from Verdi.
4. Serve with fresh semolina bread.

Increase this recipe's portions for more formal occasions. It makes a perfect reception dish for either a wedding or funeral.

Not that these two events greatly differ.

EXILES
FROM COCKAIGNE

SWADDLED IN CHEESECLOTH and wrapped in two layers of foil, three Italian sausages, which I hastily had forgotten at my parents' over Christmas, arrived by UPS at my snowbound bungalow in Syracuse, New York, on the last day of the year. Packed in a shoebox, they had traveled three hundred miles upstate—weary as the Magi—attended by two pages, a pair of fur-lined slippers. As I tried the slippers, I heralded their arrival: "All hail the three kings!"

I hummed a fanfare and removed the sausages from their box. They were indeed royalty—Abruzzese *soppressata* from Fretta Brothers in Manhattan's Little Italy. Beating a tattoo on my thigh, I slipped two sausages under my arm like swagger sticks. Using the third as a baton, I marched around the living room, a bantam on parade, followed by my wife and a procession of cats. The brass chimes rang in jubilation as I bowed before our tiny crèche.

I knelt before the stable, a reverent giant, and presented the sausages to the Christ Child. If the sausages had been smaller, or if the crèche had been larger, I would have placed them directly at Jesus' feet. But the sausages were eighteen inches long. According to the scale of the crèche, that meant each sausage to the Christ Child measured forty-five feet. What baby could eat that? I thought of another Nativity—that of Pantagruel, the son of Gargantua. According to legend, before the baby giant was born, a caravan of deli products preceded him out of his mother's womb: sixty-eight mules carrying salt blocks and baskets of peppercorns; nine dromedaries loaded with sausages, hams, jerky, and smoked tongues; seven camels packed with anchovies, sardines, creamy herring, and salted eels; twenty-four cartloads of garlic, scallions, capers, onions, roasted red peppers, and pickled artichoke hearts.

But the little tin Jesus in the manger was no giant. He was a mass-produced Christ Child in an American crèche, his stunted

23

appetite fit only for Gerber's. It was a sin, but the only thing to do with those forty-five-foot sausages was to eat them myself.

Reverently, I unwrapped the largest sausage and cut myself a slice. It was hot and spicy, but that wasn't why tears ran down my face. Three years had passed since I had last tasted such joy. Three years. That was the last Christmas I had spent with my parents and sister. Since then, I had become practically a vegetarian, for reasons that will become clearer, but here I was, a shameless carnivore again, and I ate slice after slice after slice. My smacking lips formed the magic word of my childhood: *cuc-cag-na, cuc-cag-na.*

Cuccagna means plenty, abundance, bonanza. It also means Cockaigne, the peasant paradise of medieval and Renaissance Europe that later, during the Golden Door period, became the immigrant nickname for *L'America. Cuccagna* is the Brueghel inside your mouth: the land where mountains are ricotta, rivers are wine, and spaghetti grows on trees. It is ruled by King Bugalosa, an ogre who farts manna and spits marzipans. Fish, not lice, breed in his tangled hair. Bugalosa's palace is made of cold cuts. The banners on his battlements are gigantic sausages.

My chewing slowed, and the wave of joy which had buoyed me washed out to sea. I would never taste *cuccagna* again. After nearly a century, Fretta Brothers had closed its doors forever. Four years before, exorbitant rent had forced third-generation owners Ralph and Joe Fretta to abandon their shop on the corner of Hester and Mott streets and move to Brooklyn, but on St. Anthony's Day, 1997, Fretta's announced it was going out of business. Papa raided the store and bought as many sausages as he could. These three were the last of the horde.

"*Enjoy it, Totò,*" read Papa's card. "*No more after this.*" I chewed and chewed, and it was like chewing my own heart. In that moment of full-bodied satisfaction, of reconciliation, I had tasted my death, and the death of everything I love. It wasn't a subjective reaction so much as an archeology of tastes. Time and history are literally a matter of sausages to me. They have marked the milestones of my life—not just of my individual life but my collective life as a member of a vanishing culture. Whenever I read a scholarly book that presumes to explain "the Italian American experience" through charts and statistics, I feel like I'm eating straw.

"Yes, yes, yes," I huff, "but have you tasted Abruzzese sausage lately?"

Italian Americans can learn more about the heartbreak and horror of assimilation from *soppressata* than from any book. This particular sausage has gone from being a staple, to a treat, to a delicacy, to a swindle in less than thirty years. The phenomenon is a minor tragedy in our history—a minor tragedy, but a telling one.

D URING MY CHILDHOOD, all the *salumerias,* the Italian delis in the Metropolitan area, carried Abruzzese sausages. We could find them everywhere: Manhattan, Brooklyn, Queens, Long Island, Hoboken, Neptune, Camden, Philadelphia. They were part of the pride and pageantry of the neighborhood delis. During religious holidays, the display windows resembled a Roman triumph: black and green olives arranged like foot soldiers; oil and wine flasks decorated like generals; cavalries of canned goods on Sicilian donkey carts; chariots of Parmesan cheese wheels; galleons of *mozzarella* in canals of milk; trumpets of *zamponi, cacciacavalli* and *provoloni;* triumphal arches of *prosciutti* and *mortadelle;* and finally, our standard bearers: the Abruzzese sausages. They were as proud as the statues on Easter Island, monoliths convinced of their own immortality. They never heard the admonitory fly buzzing in their ears that all glory is fleeting.

Neither did I. For me, those sausages were the food of the gods. Not a week passed without Papa bringing home a dozen batons. I ate them with Italian bread, with eggs and peas, with rappi and garlic, with cheese and olives. For special reasons, however, my favorite snack was sliced Abruzzese *soppressata* served on medallions of fresh Molisana *mozzarella.* Until 1963, Abruzzo and Molise formed a single region, a huge antipasto platter cooled by mountain breezes. Molisani neighbors supplied imported mozzarella from Isernia and Campobasso, while Abruzzese relatives provided homemade *soppressata* from the Chieti province. Dodging the health inspectors stalking trichinosis, Papa smuggled this forbidden sausage from the post office or the airport.

"Taste where you're from!" he crowed. "You'll learn why the Romans never beat us!"

Soppressata literally means compressed, so Papa's boast packs four thousand years of history into one bite. Even when Abruzzo was called Samnium, after the untamable Samnites whom Rome was forced to make citizens, the region near the Majella Mountains was fabled for its *salumen,* a mix of salted pork. In his *Natural History,* Pliny the Elder praises this primitive form of *salami* and attributes its taste to the quality of the local pigs. "No other animal furnishes more variety to the tongue," he claims. "Its meat provides nearly fifty flavors, other animals' only one." A cross between wild boars and domesticated hogs, Samnite pigs foraged in the mountain woods. They munched acorns, drank from streams, and sweetened their breath on marjoram and thyme. But besides being a prized source of pork, these free-ranging swine were a political symbol. They reminded the Caesars that Rome could not housebreak Samnium. When the Samnites became Christianized, pork retained its talismanic power. During the Middle Ages, the Abruzzesi venerated Saint Anthony of Egypt, the patron of swineherds. On his feast day, villagers shinned the *Albero della Cuccagna,* the Cockaigne Tree, a maypole festooned with salami.

My mountain relatives were almost as festive. Riotous *contadini* with thick thighs and coarse laughs, they sent me sausages wrapped in graphic but playful letters celebrating the slaughter that made their gift possible. Homer in his mock-heroic poem sings of the battle between crabs and mice. Poets in their own right, my aunts and uncles sang of the battle between peasants and pigs. It was a close battle, one in which the pigs had a fighting chance. That fact alone made their flesh wholesome. It's one thing to eat a boon companion with whom you've played and wrestled, quite another to eat a stranger whose life has been a series of degradations. Most American pigs are convicts in a mechanized gulag, but the pigs in my father's village were as colorful and flamboyant as Ariosto's knight. Don Peppe, the village doctor, whose library contained a flyspecked copy of *Orlando Furioso,* once improvised a pig epic in *ottava rima:*

> Of sows and boars, of shoats and runts, and wine-
> Soaked sucklings, I sing! This poem, San Anton',
> O patron of swineherds, is yours. Let mine
> Be the labor—and the taste!

A leathery old man with tobacco-stained teeth, a paintbush moustache, and mocking blue eyes, Don Peppe named his own pigs
Astolfo, Zerbino, Dudone, and Iroldo. Lavishing them with praise
from their infancy, he honored their last days by awarding them
colorful neckerchiefs. After butchering and curing his pigs, Don
Peppe would pick up his Ariosto, his hands still stained with gore,
and improvise more verses. Such rustic chivalry suits a province
whose flag is emblazoned with a heraldic boar.

SADLY, THESE GLORY DAYS belong to a mythic past, when
Anthony the Swineherd used a sow's whisker to steal fire from
Hell and lit my grandmother's hearth. Now I live in a Godless
present, a time of shame and famine, and my appetite is more
shrunken than the Christ Child's in the toy crèche. Too late, I
finally understand the meaning of that New Year's omen. On the
night I received my parents' care package, I dreamt I saw fifty
Abruzzese sausages, fat and huge, hanging in a *salumeria* window.
Along came fifty lean sausages—no bigger than my thumb, so
pathetically shriveled I mistook them for dried peppers—and gobbled up the fat ones.

Okay, so I plagiarized, but the USDA still prohibits the import
of Abruzzese salami, despite protests from Italian American lobby-
ists. If you crave quality *soppressata* from Columbus, Di Bruno, or
Ticino, you must resort to Williams Sonoma and Zingerman's.
Catering to the elite, these click-and-order yuppie boutiques have
trounced brick-and-mortar Italian delis, whose dwindling customer base has lowered quality and raised prices. The homemade
sausages are too dry, too fatty, or too moldy, and are always too
expensive. Even drek that could not have bribed the dregs of society fifty years ago now costs five, ten times what it used to.

Nevertheless, displaced Abruzzesi from New York's Five Boroughs still order *soppressata* from their old neighborhood stores—
sometimes from as far away as Seattle, Washington—out of loyalty
and nostalgia, if nothing else. It's a form of protest. The most miserable sausage in the shabbiest *salumeria* still beats a Big Mac.
Memories and principles, however, cannot satisfy the belly, and
the more desperate and resourceful strive to recapture the joy of
cuccagna, that rapturous sense of abundance that is the true and
only Eden. In this pursuit, even sedentary retirees display the fool-
hardy courage of Renaissance explorers.

My father's quest for *cuccagna* brought him to the wilds of northern New Jersey. By the Delaware Water Gap, an Abruzzese pig farmer makes *soppressata* the old-fashioned way. Strictly speaking, this *paisan* is not an entrepreneur. Solitary and self-sufficient, he refuses to advertise. But through word of mouth, hundreds of Abruzzesi—particularly during Christmas and Easter—knock on his door and ask for his sausages. They are indeed spectacular: lean but filling, piquant but not too hot.

"I don't cut corners," he told Papa.

Trimming the heads and necks of twenty hogs, he chops, grinds, and mixes the meat with belly and back fat. Salted and doused with red wine, the ground pork is seasoned with garlic, celery root, cloves, nutmeg, peppercorns, paprika, and a pinch of cayenne; then stuffed into a jute bag and pressed with a weight (hence the name *soppressata*). Once flattened, the salami is knotted, formed into bricks, and air-dried in a cool, dark place for forty days. Short curing makes *soppressata* softer and tastier than *capicola*, which has the advantage of being made from shoulder pork. Finally, the sausage is cut to length and carefully packed in olive-oil-filled drums. Each drum costs $200. Unflinchingly, my father paid it. So would have I.

You can't find that kind of quality in Syracuse, New York. God knows I've tried. Lombardi's on Lodi Street is one of the few vital businesses on the North Side, Salt City's Little Italy, a forlorn and desperate community violated by a brutal economy and haunted by dead dreams. There's little *cuccagna* here, God help us, but what little there is is shelved at Lombardi's. It's a family business, just treading water against Wegmans and other supermarket chains circling it like sharks, and so they are forced to cut corners, particularly when they can't move the goods. And they can't, thanks to the recession. The goods their customers crave are the very goods they can no longer afford. I know this. They know this. Everybody knows this. If Fretta's threw in the towel, what chance is there for a place like Lombardi's? Significantly, the store's interior—cozy, immaculate, well-lit—appears in the Erie Canal Museum's elegiac slideshow. ("*Time . . .*," intones E. G. Marshall, as if performing a voice-over for General Electric. "*Every moment of time makes you a part of history.*") The coroner's verdict is already in: "Death by Neglect."

These are facts. But when seeking *cuccagna*, facts are of no avail. There is only the bottomless hunger for happiness, and you become caught in self-defeating, repetitive routines. For six years, I always would ask for imported Abruzzese sausage, I always would be told they don't carry it anymore, I always would settle for the domesticated kind, and I always would choke on disappointment. It was a *bidone*, a swindle, goddamnit. A *bidone* is literally an empty oil drum used to falsify a quota or hoodwink customs. Domesticated sausages are *bidoni*. They taste like those hollow plastic sausages which now hang in the display windows of *salumerias*. The first time it happened I confronted one of the young Lombardi brothers. I can never keep them straight. They're practically twins: same hooded eyes, same Roman nose, same dark moustache.

"What the hellja sell me?" I demanded.

With infinite patience and resignation, Lombardi shrugged and spread his hands. He agreed, but what could you do? "How 'bout a free jar of olives?" he offered.

I muttered something about prostitution. To my surprise, Lombardi laughed.

"You got it, buddy," Lombardi said. "Every sausage has its pimp."

How can Italians pimp sausages? I can understand their selling innocents into slavery during the Children's Crusade, but pimping sausages? That's vile. But I've seen this prostitution with my own eyes. On Route 690 in Syracuse—just before the abandoned train station, where plaster statues commemorating past commuters resemble the human casts from Pompeii—a giant sow in a fluffy tutu leers and dances a can-can. As she entices speeding drivers to taste her proffered thigh, a billboard proclaims: "PUT A GIANELLI IN YOUR BELLY!"

When my wife first saw this sign, she muttered, "Jesus Christ, why don't they just say 'Come Pork Our Pig'?" I laughed and shook my head, a habitual reaction to America, and wondered what Don Peppe would have thought. A classicist and a devout Catholic, who knew Virgil's *Aeneid* by heart and attended daily Mass, the old man would have attributed such Neronean gaucheness to bad taste or original sin. But I'm afraid the explanation is more subtle and complicated. Sausage pimping has more to do with the processes of history and the dynamics of making it in America. It is a tale of digestion and consumption.

LIKE FOOD, history goes down the gullet of time one way. (Except, of course, when time throws up. Eternal recurrence is just another name for *agita*.) Time gobbles customs and nations more greedily than Neapolitan urchins gobble sausages. The displacements of history—wars, mass migrations, technological revolutions—are powerful digestives. Saturn devours all his children, even *salumeria* dynasties. Recipes are lost, standards warped, even in the process of trying to preserve them. The grandchildren and great grandchildren of the mighty *salumieri* of the past are not the same as their forebears. They may have the same features, use the same gestures, sell the same wares; but they are not the same people. Their eyes, though shrewd, lack the depth of experience informed by tradition. Their voices fail to resonate when they take your order. Their aprons are as white and sterile as a nurse's uniform. Their establishments are more like stage sets than butcher shops. No sweat, no sawdust, no blood, no flies.

I have been told that it is useless to complain about these things. Only the old complain, and the old are reproachful ghosts. I'm a writer and a historian, so I suppose I'm a reproachful ghost, too. But the fact is, the surest way to measure dramatic change is to notice how few people actually recognize it. Third- and fourth-generation Italian Americans relish the domestic sausages in these artificial *salumerias*. Disheartening, but unsurprising. When the last witness of *cuccagna* is silenced, when the last residue of imported sausages becomes so much slop in a nursing home bedpan, the new sausages, the fake ones, will then taste delicious. No one will be around to refute them. Meanwhile, shopping at a *salumeria* has become a painful and alienating experience. It's like watching a Palladian villa being converted into a Holiday Inn.

For my parents and grandparents, the names Sbarro and Fretta were as meaningful and inspiring as the names Medici and Visconti—more meaningful, more inspiring, because their greatness derived from feeding, not murdering people. Unlike art and politics, food is a shared power. The names of those *salumieri* were the coat of arms of three generations of immigrants. But they aren't names anymore, and they aren't ours. They are logos belonging to Madison Avenue. You see them in supermarkets and malls, on billboards dotting the highways. It is the fate of many Italian names, high and low, in the marketplace of history. A descendant of Lorenzo de Medici writes upscale cookbooks. You can buy them at Williams-Sonoma in the Syracuse Carousel Mall. Sbarro is now a fast-food franchise like McDonald's. You can eat there, if you like, at the mall food court. The way of all flesh is through the meat grinder of history. Patrician or plebeian, Italians are so many sausages to be sold.

Unfortunately, we cannot cry foul. We have brought this degradation upon ourselves. Turning sausages into tubes, names into labels were our way of assimilating into America. I can think of few ethnic groups during the great wave of immigration who were more materialistic, more aware of, obsessed by, the economic dimension of life than we Italians. It is an ancient trait. Those tough-minded Romans had a proverb: *Ubi panis, ibi patris.* Wherever there is bread, there is your country. They could just have easily have said, wherever there are sausages. Economic necessity, not political idealism, drove the majority of our grand-parents and great-grandparents to these shores—a raw, blind, animal hunger born of centuries of poverty and disillusionment.

Our ancestors had no stomach for politics. Politics for them was a gigantic hollow sausage. The Risorgimento, Italy's War of Unification, that operatic fiasco of the mid–nineteenth century, had depleted and demoralized the rural South.

Sicilians still tell the story of Signor O. O., an old peasant from Messina. One day, Garibaldi and his Red Shirts were passing through the area and found Signor O. O. resting in the shade of a carob tree, chewing dry sausage like cud. The general, resplendent in his uniform, reined in his horse and exhorted the old man. "Rouse yourself, grandfather!" he cried. "How can you nod and chew pork in the shade when your country needs you?!" The old peasant slowly raised his stubbly chin, a gesture of Olympian indifference, and continued chewing sausage. Garibaldi, the champion of democracy, spurred his horse and trotted on. If Garibaldi had asked Signor O. O. to fight for sausages instead of democracy, the old man gladly would have presented arms. The same was true of almost an entire generation of immigrants. They came here because they wanted better sausages, not a better democracy.

L'America was the New Cockaigne. The Statue of Liberty was not a symbol of freedom but a figure on a giant wedding cake. Grub first, then rights. Those foolish enough to entertain political illusions quickly learned otherwise when they were stacked in tenements like salami. Still, more often than not, there was steady work, and that was really what these immigrants craved. A full pocket meant a full pantry, a full pantry meant a full heart. That was *cuccagna*. No wonder so many Italians based their self-esteem on food.

Food was currency, food was clout, food was stocks and bonds. The pantry was the family safe, and sausages and cold cuts were the family jewels. Good meat has always been scarce in Southern Italy, but the immigrants from that region a century ago hoarded sausages like bullion. "Money in the bank," my Abruzzese grandfather Carlo used to say. This fetish for meat was literally money in the bank for the *salumieri*. From the turn of the century to the dawn of the sixties, they prospered like lords. And why not? Didn't they deserve it? They were the heroes of the neighborhood, the ambassadors of Cockaigne.

But let's not be sentimental. They were also tough businessmen and shrewd operators. Their butcher ancestors perished in the flames of Pompeii because they were too greedy to close shop after Vesuvius exploded. ("Ya never know, honey. Someone might wanna fry bacon over that volcano.") Nevertheless, they respected their customers and were true connoisseurs of sausage. As long as the *salumieri* were rich, but not too rich; as long as their mostly Italian clientele could hold them to the highest standards, everyone, including the sausages, profited from the arrangement. Custom and tradition were partly responsible for this happy symbiosis, this delicate system of checks and balances. They also resulted from a localized economy, which continually replenished the community. We never realized that. Nothing stays localized for long in America, least of all Italian sausages. Not when there are millions of dollars in profits to be made.

BLAME ETTORE BOIARDI, better known as Chef Boy-Ar-Dee. Yes, Virginia, there really was a Chef Boy-Ar-Dee. He called himself that because even his own salesmen couldn't pronounce his name. "Everyone is proud of his family name," he later explained, "but sacrifices are necessary for progress."

Boiardi was all for progress, and he certainly was willing to sacrifice. He was head chef at Cleveland's Hotel Winton during the early twenties. Before that he had been a renowned caterer. He had even done Woodrow Wilson's wedding reception at the Hotel Greenbrier in West Virginia. I wonder if Boiardi would have cooked so well if he had known how much the future president despised Italians, how he had written a paper—while he was chancellor of Princeton—arguing that Italians were subhuman, and would later snub Orlando at the Paris Peace Conference. Perhaps Boiardi knew and didn't care. He was an ambitious young man who wanted to work for himself. A Northerner from Piacenza, perhaps he was a born capitalist.

In 1924 Boiardi opened Il Giardino d'Italia, one of Cleveland's first Italian restaurants. Actually, it was more a research lab than a restaurant. Boiardi was fascinated and disgusted by the way most of his American customers ate. He studied them. God, they were impatient. Even the wealthiest of them swilled down his food, indifferent to the time and effort that had gone into each dish. Boiardi seethed for years, but he kept right on observing. It must have been a struggle. There were probably times he contemplated poisoning the lot of them. If only he had. It would have been more forgivable. Slowly, stealthily, fantasies of revenge became dreams of avarice. Why not create Italian food that can be eaten quickly and conveniently? There must be plenty of money in that.

He broke ground in the late thirties. In a tiny loft near the restaurant, Boiardi experimented with a three-gallon vat of tomato sauce and different kinds of spaghetti, meatballs, and sausages. When he had perfected a formula, he expanded. He went through four different processing plants but wanted a location closer to local tomato growers. He found an abandoned silk mill in the farmland near Milton, Pennsylvania. Boiardi transformed the mill into a factory and gave contracts to local farmers for one thousand acres of tomatoes. That was the birth of Chef Boy-Ar-Dee.

Boiardi was not the first Italian American to mass produce ethnic food. The Ghirardellis of Frisco were turning out assembly-line Milanese chocolates, and the Fontanas of Del Monte were canning fruits and vegetables by the tons in Napa Valley. Nor was Boiardi's smug, avuncular face the first Italian icon of American junk food. Amedeo Obici in 1917 had created Mr. Peanut, who was supposed to be a Milanese man-about-town, and the Pollio family had transformed their name into Polly-O the Ricotta Parrot. But it was Boiardi, more than anyone else, who made Italian food acceptable to mainstream white America, who prostituted *cuccagna* for the sake of profit and mass appeal. Boiardi did the impossible: he turned Cockaigne into Disneyland. The guy was Faust—diabolically lucky. At first his products were only popular in the Cleveland area, but a fluke catapulted him into national prominence.

Boiardi's brother Paolo maitre d'ed at New York's Plaza Hotel. Two of his regulars, Mr. and Mrs. John Hartford, owned the Atlantic and Pacific Tea Company: the A&P supermarket chain. One afternoon the Hartfords arrived at the Plaza for lunch. They were in the mood for Italian food, but they had only ten minutes. Could Paolo prepare something for them? Paolo had some of Ettore's canned goods in the back. In five minutes the Hartfords were feasting on spaghetti and sausages—at least, it seemed like spaghetti and sausages to them. They were so impressed that they enshrined Ettore Boiardi's face in supermarket shelves across the country.

The sausages had done it. Didn't I tell you history is a matter of sausages? Boiardi became so famous that when World War II broke out, the government buttonholed him to create better army rations. Trainloads of supplies pulled into his plant in Milton, and Boiardi converted car after car of ham and eggs into mess for the troops. He also found a new market for his products. Apparently, the War Department could live with that. On June 14, 1943, on a national broadcast, the Army Quartermaster Corp awarded Boiardi the coveted E Pennant for his achievements. He went on to become a multimillionaire. Ironically, the war created the national market for Italian convenience food. The boys couldn't get enough of it. According to the neighborhood cynics, the GIs slaughtered like pigs at Anzio had given their lives for Chef Boy-Ar-Dee.

But Italian sausages are even easier to mass produce than precooked pasta dishes. The *salumerias* discovered this in the postwar years, when they went corporate. The Italian American exodus to the suburbs, which had begun in the mid-fifties, had created a radical demographic shift. Needing new subjects, the sausage kings created a game plan: *Remarket, repackage. Eliminate the middle man. Cut your losses. Turn liabilities into assets.* The most successful *salumieri* invested in agribusiness. What they did, and still do, to their pigs would have made their grandfathers weep.

Here's how you make Abruzzese sausage today: Herd millions of pigs into stifling, filthy warehouses. Cram thirty or forty of them into twenty foot square pens. Force them to breathe ammoniated air and to eat their own shit. Snip off their tails to prevent cannibalism. When a sow farrows, incapacitate it in a metal crate. Imprison her young in wire battery cages, or better, to save space, flat pans stacked three tiers high. Never allow the piglets to nestle directly against their mother. Instead, let them strain to suckle her teats through iron bars. Deprive them of sunlight. Gorge them with trash. Stuff them with steroids. Humiliate them in death. Dismantle their bodies like old jalopies. Then, when you've ground their rubberized flesh into pulp, boast that you only use the best spices to give your sausages that "authentic" taste.

MY NEIGHBORS, the Onondaga Indians, believe a hunter must honor his prey and kill it cleanly and swiftly. If not, he will feed its fear and suffering to his family. Don Peppe, my relatives, and their Abruzzese neighbors also understood this principle and treated their pigs with respect. It was a way of respecting themselves—and their ancestors. After all, Don Peppe claimed, Father Aeneas founded Alba Longa, the mother city of Rome, on a site where an enormous white sow had farrowed and nursed thirty piglets. By contrast, American pigs die a prolonged death in the *salumeria* factories. Confinement and immobility, stress and poor diet create the most horrible diseases: arthritis, lameness, tics, seizures, diabetes, kidney failure, hernia, cardiovascular problems. Working-class Italians, who never made their million in America and who perish in dead-end neighborhoods like Syracuse's Northside, share the same symptoms. We literally are what we eat.

But commercial hype and misplaced pride prevent us from seeing that. We are prisoners of Madison Avenue. Through nostalgia and misdirection, advertisers convince us that horror is *cuccagna,* that plastic tubes are actually sausages. They cannibalize Italian art and history to promote Americanized *salumerias.* Surreal portraits, like those of Arcimboldo (human heads composed entirely of meats), hang on shop walls. Magazine ads for cold cuts resemble the still lifes of Bergamo, the Renaissance city whose artists specialized in painting food. Replicas of Porcellino, the bronze boar who is one of the mascots of Florence, adorn salami displays in supermarkets. Marc Anthony Foods of Syracuse, New York—*Et tu, paisan?*—uses the chaplet of the Caesars to promote *soppressata.* ("Friends, Romans, countrymen," reads an ad, "lend me your sausages!") It is a postmodern Saturnalia, the Roman Festival of Saturn, where time devours its tail and tragedy degenerates into farce in a great end-of-the-year blow-out.

I discuss these matters with my Abruzzese father, a perceptive and articulate man whose retirement from Seventh Avenue has made him philosophical about the immigrant experience. He agrees that America has become a nightmare but argues that, until recently, Italians had been able to sustain their own culture. It had remained *Cosa Nostra,* our thing. I shake my head and tell him about the 1893 Chicago World's Fair.

To celebrate the quadricentennial of Columbus's voyage to America, Italian immigrants cleared six hundred acres of prairie muck in Jackson Park and constructed exhibits reflecting a glorious heritage: Roman colonnades, Florentine cupolas, Baroque fountains of tritons and mermaids, Venetian canals with actual gondolas, Neapolitan coffee houses, Sicilian donkey carts. They even built a replica of St. Peter's, reduced to one sixteenth its size. Filthy, sweaty, backbreaking work, and even in the subzero January and February weather, the Italians went shirtless and often became dehydrated. But they were proud of those exhibits, and they were relieved to escape the stink and squalor of the stockyards. It was a hell for pigs. The din alone haunted them. Thirteen years later, in *The Jungle,* Upton Sinclair called this sound "the hog squeal of the universe."

On Columbus Day the Italian workmen brought their families to the Fair. Most chose to take the steamer from downtown because it was a way of coming to American again—but this time on their own terms. When the White City loomed in the distance, with its turrets and gazebos and Ferris wheel, the children clapped and shouted. "*Cuccagna!*" they squealed. Cockaigne, Cockaigne! The men squeezed their wives' waists and pointed. You see? We brought *Italia* to these shores. Carrying small Italian flags and wearing red, white, and green ribbons, the families disembarked onto a mechanical sidewalk and purchased maps. They toured the exhibitions and marveled at a ten-ton block of Wisconsin cheese; a thirty-five-foot high display of Napa Valley oranges, topped with a bronze eagle; an eighteen- by twenty-four-foot map of the United States made entirely of pickles, vinegar, and spices.

In their grandparents' day, such spectacles of abundance had been organized for the aristocracy's amusement. Staged during Corpus Christi, these festivals were called *Cuccagnas*. In Naples and Palermo, the Bourbons stockpiled produce and livestock in the cathedral square, invited the poor to grab as much as they could, set fire to the pyramid of goods, and laughed at the burnt and the maimed. *L'America*, however, was the true *Cuccagna*. Its abundance belonged to all who worked hard.

With renewed faith and whetted appetites, the Italians visited the Midway and gorged themselves on sausages, courtesy of the Wellington Catering Company, which had butchered fifty hogs that morning to honor Columbus. And such wonderful sausages! Sweet sausages, hot sausages, dry sausages, smoked sausages, sausages packed with fennel or caraway, liver sausages stuffed with orange zest. There was even Abruzzese *soppressata*, almost as good as the Old Country. The families were so busy devouring pork, so busy basking in ethnic pride, so busy riding the Ferris wheel or humming along as the band played the *Gazza Ladra Overture* that they failed to notice things. They never realized they were barred from the classier exhibits; never knew Italy had been blackballed from the fair; never eavesdropped as Senator Thomas Wetherell Palmer, Commissioner of the World's Columbian Exposition, told the U.S. ambassador to Italy: "Our exhibits are better than the real thing. Know why? No wops!"

To honor the workers, South Side contractors and Pullman porters composed a song:

After the Fair is over,
What will the Dagos do?

But the fair continues every time we Italians open our wallets and purses. As Ricky Roma, the hustling realtor in *Glengarry Glen Ross,* observes: "It's a carnival out there, my friend!" A staged carnival, in which we are tourists, not natives. For souvenirs, we buy Sbarro T-shirts. We read packaging like guide books (*"Contains pork, salt, spices, dextrose, sodium erythorbate, lactic acid, sodium nitrate, sodium nitrite, and"*—how's this for symbolism?—*"starter culture"*) because we can't find our way around our guts. Sirens bewitch us. Television, the electronic Cockaigne, beckons, beckons. *"Abbondanza!"* blurt the announcers. Claymation sausages cavort to Rossini. In San Giorgio commercials, spaghetti grows on trees—just like in the old folk tales.

I KNOW THIS GAME from the inside. I've worked in television. I've worked in advertising. I've pimped a sausage or two in my time. I wrote copy for butchers, caterers, restaurateurs, franchisers. So many were Italian Americans, who expected special treatment from me. After all, a goombah knows what sells. One radio spot I produced for a Newark deli still appalls me.

At the time, Hormel had appropriated Lewis Hines' classic photo study of Ellis Island for a television campaign. A montage of bearded men and shawled women, followed by a shimmering landscape of amber waves of grain, promoted the purity of Homeland Hard Salami. Besotted, the deli owner wanted me to create "something exactly the same, only different." I tried my damnedest to dissuade him, even quoting the Hormel motto: *"Innovate, don't imitate."* But the client insisted. He wanted me to compare the immigrant experience to his cold cuts.

I didn't miss a thing: the swelling music, the sound effects of gulls and waves. The bland copy lumped together all Italian immigrants, reducing their regional differences to ground pork. (Forgive me, Don Peppe.) The announcer was perfect. He sounded like a well-meaning health inspector at Ellis Island. When I emerged from the recording studio, I swiped a paperweight from a secretary's desk and demolished my typewriter—but not before pecking out and posting the following pasquinade:

Give me your ham and *prosciutto!*
Your huddled sausage yearning to be free!
Your *capicolla* no one else will eat!
Send all these stomach-tossed to me!
I lift my lamp beside the Golden Arches!

Like the sword of the angel, those Golden Arches forever bar our way back to Eden.

I ATE THE THREE Christmas sausages my mother sent me in less than forty-eight hours. It was a desperate act. But I belong to a desperate people. Italian Americans are exiles from Cockaigne, and our lives are an endless Lent without sausages. We seldom stare down the throat of that emptiness, because capitalism convinces us we have succeeded. We spend our money, don't we? We get our three squares. Munching sausage rolls, we swagger through the mall and boast how our own Manny De Bartolo practically created shopping centers in 1948. Or we drop in at Pizza Hut, as a kind of joke, and order a three-cheese pizza topped with sausages. We pretend soft drinks are wine and toast Roger Enrico, the former CEO of Pepsi Cola. To the Real Thing!

But it's not the real thing. Poking the rubber mulch on our pizza, we can't fathom our grief. No problem. Over the speakers Ol' Blue Eyes soothes us with "My Way": "*I chewed it up, and spit it out . . .*" We have connived with invisible forces to undo ourselves. *They* chew us up. *They* spit us out. The Pizza Hut walls are decorated with bogus tintypes of bogus immigrants, forgeries of pictures from our grandparents' album: the village blacksmith, the village cobbler, the village crabber, the village birdcatcher. We are not producers but products. That's what happens at the power lunch of America. You need a long spoon to eat with the Devil; ours wasn't long enough. We chew our plastic and wait to die.

When our consumers are finally through with us, when we are nothing but a heap of empty sausage skins, they will bulldoze us into a mass grave, and that will be the end. Should you wish to mourn us then, bring no flowers, give no eulogy, light no candle. Instead, place a wreath of Abruzzese sausages on our grave—the real ones, please—and press your ear against the ground. You will hear the lips of the dead smack the syllables *cuc-cag-na, cu-cag-na, cuc-cag-na, cuc-cag-na . . .*

PRIMO

*Calabrian
Onion Soup*

Tears and Onions

CALABRIAN
ONION SOUP

ITALIAN CHEFS USE ONIONS sparingly, because of their stink and association with poverty. Short of a bomb threat, nothing will clear a Neapolitan pizzeria faster than an *Americano* ordering a pie with extra onions.

Consequently, Italian cuisine has no equivalent for French onion soup, but this Calabrian recipe comes close. Bucking the region's traditional austerity, it calls for a touch of sugar and a shot of grappa. For a less fiery, more elegant taste, substitute dry Marsala or sherry.

INGREDIENTS
- 2 ½ to 3 pounds large Vidalia onions, sliced thin
- 6 tablespoons olive oil
- 2 teaspoons sea salt
- 1 tablespoon sugar
- 8 cups organic beef stock
- 6 tablespoons grappa or ¼ cup dry Marsala or sherry
- 1 loaf baguette bread, cut into ½-inch slices
- Grated Pecorino Romano cheese

DIRECTIONS
1. In a deep sauce pan, sauté the onions in the olive oil until they begin to brown.
2. Season with salt and sugar. (If using Marsala or sherry, add now!)
3. Heat the beef stock to boiling in a large pot. Slowly pour the broth over onions, cover the pan, reduce heat, and simmer for half hour.
4. Stir in grappa and cook another 5 minutes.
5. Meanwhile, heat oven to 350 degrees. Place sliced bread on baking tray and toast until golden brown.

6. Divide toasted bread among bowls and ladle soup on
   top. Serve with grated cheese.

Supposedly, this soup increases longevity. That might have less to
do with its antitoxin nutrients than with your breath's affect on
the Angel of Death.

TEARS AND ONIONS

"LIFE IS AN ONION," Nonna Agata used to say. *"You can't peel it without tears."* This rueful proverb, repeated often during my childhood, haunts me whenever I prepare onions. No matter how often I steal myself, no matter how often I am reassured by the homey objects in my kitchen—the Arts and Crafts cabinets, the red Formica counter, the Cutco knife set, the Amish cutting board, the wooden plaque from Monte Cassino with the words *"Dacci Oggi il Nostro Pane Quotidiano"* (Give us this day our daily bread)—I weep uncontrollably whenever I peel onions. My eyes don't water so much as spurt, and for five overwhelming seconds, the world consists of nothing but tears and onions.

Until recently, having grown up in a Jersey suburb instead of a Sicilian village, I found no comfort in my grandmother's wisdom. If anything, it made me feel more alienated and un-American. America is the land of happiness, after all, where memory should be a colorful slide show of Kodak moments, not a meditation on sorrow. If you don't believe me, consider how middle-class Americans prepare onions. With their Ronco® peelers and dicers, they skin, quarter, and mince bulbs like magic, with no mess or tears. Those television chefs are even worse. Dressed in sterile white aprons, speaking with the monotonic enthusiasm of a NASA official promoting the next space shuttle, they try convincing you that onions actually *can* be peeled without tears.

Well, I've consulted all the WASP cookbooks, from Fannie Farmer to Martha Stewart, and none of the suggestions work—not peeling onions under cold running water, not packing them in ice, not using a small fan. I am forever crying at my cutting board, much to the chagrin of my wife and friends, who sometimes catch me stifling a sob. When they ask what's the matter, I repeat my grandmother's proverb: "Life is an onion. You can't peel it without tears."

Nonna certainly knew about tears and onions. Even in her nineties, when her hands were gnarled roots and her face resembled a haggard lioness's, she could peel onions all day, ten, fifteen pounds at a time. Her expression was always stoic, but the tears streamed like a fountain from her clouded blue eyes, and the onions piled higher than Mount Etna. Although she always peeled more onions than we possibly could use, she was neither senile nor crazy. She was simply used to cooking for lots of people, whether it was the large clan in her crowded Bay Ridge apartment or those thirty sharecroppers back in Sicily, where she had owned and managed olive and citrus groves.

Nonna's property had included an onion field, which proved invaluable when feeding the men. Meat, always scarce and tough in Sicily, was doubly so during the war, and Nonna tenderized hunks of beef and mutton in vats of onions. Miraculously, leathery meat would soften, tasteless meat would become savory, meat on the verge of spoiling would revive. In her prime, Nonna peeled mountains of onions to secure her land and her children's love. In her dotage, she peeled mountains of onions to mourn their loss.

I vividly remember her last peeling marathon. It was May 13, 1981, the day John Paul II was shot. "On the Feast of Our Lady of Fatima!" Nonna wailed. "It's the end of the world!" She was upset enough already. At the time, she was nursing my semi-invalid mother, her youngest and favorite daughter, who had suffered another attack of spinal arthritis. For two straight weeks, Mamma would scream all night from pain. Nonna and I hadn't slept in days, so we were particularly distressed by the shooting. For comfort, she peeled onions at the patio table, while I sat beside her with my Remington and typed on onion skin, the only available paper in the house. The letters came out like Braille. Nonna shook her head and grumbled. If Vatican security had heeded the prophecies of Fatima, the Holy Father would never have been harmed.

Concerned, I stopped typing and helped with the peeling. We sat silently and listened to the jays and redwings. Nonna worked grimly, relentlessly, never breaking her rhythm. Suddenly, her face twitching, she snatched an onion and peeled it to the core.

"You see?" she spat. "That's what life does to us!"

Yes, I thought. Layer by layer, it strips us clean. I considered everything Nonna had lost in America: her health, from sunless sweatshops and ammonia-scented bathrooms; her money, siphoned by her good-for-nothing husband to prevent her from returning to Sicily; her children, most of whom had betrayed and abandoned her. Back in Villabate, a prosperous suburb of Palermo, she had been a queen, albeit a beleaguered one. Her large farm was only the vestige of a once vast plantation.

Nonna's family was originally Spanish gentry, who came with the viceroys in the late seventeenth century and lived in Bagheria before settling in Villabate. Over time, the property they had received from the Bourbons was whittled away, first by the English constitution after the Napoleonic wars, which outlawed primogeniture and broke up Sicily's huge estates, then by the Garibaldini during the Risorgimento. What wasn't vandalized by the unions or plundered by the Fascists was incinerated by the Americans in April, 1943, when Palermo and its environs were carpet-bombed.

But Nonna remained indomitable. During Operation Husky, the Allied invasion of Sicily, she visited the headquarters of the Seventh Army when it was stationed in Palermo and, through a translator, spoke to one of Patton's staff officers. Any soldier, she announced, who molested one of her farm girls would be castrated. She would see to it, personally. Life could not take her pride, but it took everything else, and she was forced to seek asylum in the country of her destroyers.

"We are all onions in the hands of God," she said.

I nodded but said nothing. At twenty-one, I thought the analogy was farfetched. Onions in the hands of a hungry God? Not exactly the title of a Jonathan Edwards sermon. But at fifty, after witnessing my fair share of tragedies, Nonna's words make perfect sense. Sometimes I wonder if that's why I handle onions so gingerly. Maybe if I treat onions gently, God, all evidence to the contrary, will treat me gently, too. A little sympathetic magic to ward off the evil eye.

Nonna's fetish for onions was rooted in antiquity. Of all of Italy's regional cuisines, Sicily's is closest to that of classical Rome, where the onion, indispensable to kitchen and dispensary, was revered as a powerful talisman. Those who wanted their affairs to go well wore an onion amulet on the Kalends of May. This custom persists in Sicily, where onions are kept in one's pocket on *Caldendimaggio,* May Day. Onions bring good luck. Leek Green, after all, was the most successful chariot team in the Coliseum, its winners showered with scallion confetti. Onions even the odds, whether you are embarking on a new venture or a new journey. When I first left for college, Nonna advised me to carry an onion in my suitcase. Bulbous and self-contained, yet renewing itself and growing from within, the onion is the herb of both stability and change. According to Ovid, Glaucus the fisherman was transformed into a sea god by eating chives sprouting near the shore.

Like the ancient Romans, my grandmother was a pagan materialist. If Lucretius considered the atom the fundamental building block of the universe, Nonna thought it was the onion. So when she told me life is an onion bulb, she meant it literally as well as figuratively—a proposition with existential implications. If life is an onion, then so are you. My father drove home this point when I was a boy. This was after we had moved from Brooklyn to Freehold, New Jersey, and I was having an obligatory identity crisis. Alienated in junior high, I was obsessed with finding my true self.

"What true self?" Papa asked. As a former shepherd, now a production manager on Seventh Avenue, he didn't take much stock in true selves. Unlike Nonna, he loved America precisely because it had allowed him to transform himself. But then, he was originally from the Abruzzi, Ovid's region. Normally, Papa was impatient with me, but he had finished hoeing the backyard garden, his chief delight, and was whistling and washing mud off his hands. In his rare merry moods, he always humored his bewildering mooncalf of a son who read too many books. "What true self?" he repeated.

"You know," I mumbled. "The real me. The one deep down inside."

"I see," Papa said, suppressing a smirk. "So you're looking for the pearl in the onion."

I squinted an eye. "Onions have pearls?"

"Sure," Papa said. "Haven't you heard of pearl onions?"

"Yeah."

"Well, that's the kind with the pearl. Mamma and I bought you one at Brock's Market this morning. We could see you were upset, so we got you a present." And he handed me what looked like a huge, filthy Spanish onion. "Okay," he instructed, "now peel it carefully, one layer at a time. Don't use a knife, use your hands. That way you won't damage the pearl."

So I peeled the onion, layer by layer, for what seemed an eternity. Grit got under my nails, in my nostrils, between my teeth. Juice coated and burned my palms till they were numb and sticky. My eyes stung, my throat gagged, my chest tightened, but I was determined to find that pearl. Finally, through a veil of tears, I reached the center of the onion . . . a perfect void. No pearl.

"Let that be lesson to you, *scimunito*," Papa said, with customary sternness. "An onion's just an onion, all the way through. There's no pearl. If you want a pearl for an onion, take a look at this, 'cause it's the only pearl onion there is." And between his thumb and forefinger, he held a delicate, opalescent bulb, no bigger than a robin's egg. "You see? You can eat this. You can soak it in a marinade, mix it in a preserve, or stuff it in a bird. So the next time you wanna know if something's true, ask yourself if you can eat it. That's all life is, son. Either it's an onion or it's nothing."

I pondered these words: Exactly *how* is life like an onion? Is it a series of discrete moments covering a void, all skin and no core? Is it nothing but the sum of your experiences and relationships with nothing beyond, before, or behind it? These are questions for postmodern philosophers and Buddhist monks. As a writer, historian, and cook, I venture only this: memory, the mother of all culture, is a series of diaphanous layers, not unlike the translucent strata of an onion, and this layering flavors our personality and outlook the way a shallot flavors a sauce. That is why, in my case, onions enhance recollection. One whiff brings back more memories than Proust's madeleine.

As a boy, I often accompanied Mamma to the open air markets in Bensonhurst and helped her shop for the best onions. The smell exhilarated me, and I loved showing off for the neighborhood men by lifting the ten-pound mesh bags. Sometimes Mamma bought onions that came from a place with the magical name Canastota. "Is that where covered wagons are made?" I once asked.

The Sicilian grocer laughed and said. "That's Conestoga. This is Canastota. Onion Town, kid. Ain't you ever heard of Onion Town?"

"Is everyone there an onion?" I asked, and the shoppers guffawed.

"It's upstate," explained the grocer, a stocky, unshaven man with tobacco-stained teeth. "Beautiful place. I got family there. Lots of *paesani*."

Mamma nodded and said we had relatives near Onion Town, the children of Nonna's brother, Great Uncle Gian, who lived in Utica. I pursed my lip and waddled after her. I was sure she was telling the truth, but I preferred imagining an enchanted village of onions, where everyone was named Cipolla or Vidalia. The real history of Onion Town, however, is far more fabulous.

LOCATED BETWEEN Syracuse and Utica, Canastota, New York, once produced most of the onions in the Northeast, but its legendary mucklands, primarily cultivated by Sicilian immigrants and their children, are not a natural phenomenon. Like almost everything else in Onion Town, the rich soil is a product of the Erie Canal, which transformed Canastota, incorporated in 1835, from a backwards hamlet to a prosperous town with four railroad lines and factories that manufactured cut glass, coaster and dump wagons, and steerable sleds. In fact, when the village was first settled in 1810, the mucklands didn't even exist. They were submerged under an enormous swamp stretching three miles north of the village, a Stygian tangle of trees, roots, and mud that flooded so often the settlers were obliged to build their first houses on stilts. A year later, a plank path was built through the swamp to connect Canastota to Oneida Lake, followed by an Indian trail, but the Oneidas avoided the area unless the season was very dry.

Although some early Canastotans had the foresight to see agricultural potential in this slough, canal engineers made that dream a reality. Gentleman venturers with a classical bent, they tackled the problem with the methodicalness of a Frontinius. In 1850, Douglas Ditch was cut between the swamp and Oneida Lake and twice extended in 1867 and 1875 to form a line between Sullivan and Lenox townships. Twelve years later, State Highway Commissioner Charles Foster decided that the whole area should be drained and converted into productive farmland, a project more ambitious than the Emperor Claudius's draining of the

Fucine Lake. After winning the skeptical town's approval, he began constructing what was to become Onion Town Road.

The incentive to cultivate the land, however, was spurred by the depression of 1893. After the local economy collapsed, Canastotans sought other ways to make money, so they sluiced, cleared, and tilled the bog north of the village, between Main Street and South Bay, and constructed houses and barns. The work was backbreaking and frustrating, so it is no surprise they had put it off for fifty years. Since horses were helpless in the swampy land, ditches had to be dug almost entirely by hand. Thick patches of trees, small bushes, and tangled roots still remained, and stumps had to be dynamited. Even then, many patches had poor drainage, and during the wet season, some crops were always under water. The first muck farmers were Americans, who would not stay the course. The work seemed dirty and degrading, a comedown from the village's recent glory days. But for the Italian immigrants who succeeded them, working the muck was like clearing the Promised Land.

First came the Genovese. Domenico and Assumpta Cervasco moved to the village in 1886. They operated a peanut stand on the banks of the canal off the Peterboro Street Bridge and convinced friends and relatives to join them. The Sicilians arrived a decade later. As manual laborers for the Lehigh Valley, West Shore, and New York Central Railroads, they dead-ended in Canastota and had nowhere else to go. They lived in abandoned railroad cars on the edge of town and foraged for dandelion greens. Factory work was scarce because of the depression. Fortunately, the newcomers' arrival coincided with the village's push to cultivate the mucklands.

While the Sicilians recognized this opportunity, they were reluctant to embrace it. Most had abandoned agriculture, having become thoroughly disillusioned with the soil. "Who tends the earth tends his grave," they said. Back in Sicily, they had not been *contadini*, peasants who owned and worked their own fields and vineyards, or *fittivali*, tenant farmers, or even *mezzadri*, sharecroppers, but *cafone*, unskilled farm hands and migrant pickers. The equivalent of white trash, they had lost all love for the land. It was the ancient curse of Sicily.

Twenty-five centuries of colonialism had transformed Ceres' island from the garden of the Mediterranean, where even the keenest bloodhounds would lose a scent because of the abundant flowers and herbs, into a lunar rock. The Carthaginians, to punish the Sicilians for their loyalty to the Greeks, burned wheat fields and sowed salt in the earth. The Romans, who conquered the Carthaginians, overworked the soil to feed their gluttony. The Arabs, their successors, introduced irrigation and citrus farming but also brought goats, which munched their way through the greenery. The Normans, who expelled the Arabs, deforested the island to create their fleets and composed chivalric epics while the topsoil washed away. The Spanish, who kept the best fields for themselves, were worthless, irresponsible landlords, but the Bourbons, at least, would not tax livestock, produce, and draft animals. After the revolution, however, the new Italian government taxed all three, wrecking Sicily's agriculture and sparking the Fasci riots of the 1880s. In the wake of this chaos, Sicilian peasants were faced with a stark choice: emigration or starvation. Little wonder, then, that most of Canastota's newest arrivals had sworn off farming.

But the vast mucklands seduced them. They were a return to the Golden Age. Never before had the Sicilians seen such miraculous soil. Black, rich, moist. Anything could grow in it: cabbage, chicory, celery; above all, onions. The onions tantalized them. Back in the Old Country, the man who owned an onion patch was a king. What were the glories of Segesta and Agrigento, those Grecian temples and peristyles, compared to a fertile onion patch? This attitude still prevails in Sicily, where as recently as 1975 an outraged farmer near Palazzalo Acreìde defaced a priceless Attic frieze on his property because tourists and archeologists would trample his onions to see it.

The *Americani* had their priorities straight. No ruins, just onions. And such onions! As big as your fist. Hell, bigger than the head of your first born! The Canastotans were rightly proud of them and gave them the sonorous names of race horses: Bronze Fiesta, Ebenezer, Golden Beauty, Southport White Globe. A carillon of bulbs in a paradise of onions! And if the *Americani*, with their haphazard, heavy-handed methods, could work such miracles, what might the Sicilians do, with their thousand tried-and-true, subtle techniques of coaxing crops from the dust? They gladly became sharecroppers in the American onion fields.

At first, the immigrants stuck to their old ways. The Americans were the lords, they were the vassals. They rose before dawn and walked six miles to the mucklands, carrying two loaves of bread, one for lunch, one for dinner, and did not return until well after dusk. The Americans were impressed but baffled by the way the Sicilians took to the muck. *'U fangu,* they called it. Mud. Despite the grueling sixteen-hour days, the broiling sun, the vicious horse flies and mosquitoes from Cowasselon and Canastota creeks, the Sicilians kneaded, caressed, and kissed the thick black loam. The Americans, mostly stern Presbyterians, were taken aback. This seemed more like an orgy than manual labor.

The Sicilians needed that ardor. The mucklands stretched three miles north to south, ten miles east to west, and required constant care. This cosmos of peat so impressed the immigrants that they made up stories about it, some adapted from the folk tales back home. In these tales, Christ plays a transplanted Sicilian landlord, lean and refined, who owns an infinite onion field, while stocky St. Peter guards the gate to the property and supervises the work . . .

ONE DAY JESUS is reviewing the accounts and sees Peter moping at the door. "Peter," he asks, "why so down in the mouth?"

"Lord," says Peter, "it's like this. Here I am in heaven with a fine job and a full belly. Switching from fishing to onion farming was the smartest move I made. I got a nice nest egg and feast on porgy and chives every night. But all the while, Lord, my poor mother stews in hell. Granted, she was a scold and a miser and a bit too eager with the strap. But still, a mother is a mother, and I can't stand the thought of her suffering."

Mothers are the Lord's soft spot, of course, since he dotes on the Madonna. "Hmm," he says, stroking his chin. "Normally, I don't like to bend the rules. If I did, everybody would want their relatives here, and heaven would be hell in no time. But since, thanks to you, we've had such a good harvest, it would be petty not to make an exception this once."

And he smiles and opens the great ledger book, finds the entry for Peter's mother, and runs his bony finger down the debit and credit columns. The Lord furrows his brow.

"Peter," he says, "this is going to be harder than I thought. As far as I can tell, the only decent thing your mother ever did in her life was give a leek to a beggar. That certainly doesn't merit Paradise."

"But, Lord," says Peter, *"didn't you say that if something is done for the least of your brethren, it's done for you?"*

"True, Peter. It was done for me. And it just so happens I have that leek right here." And he opens a file cabinet drawer and pulls out a splendid leek. *"My,"* says the Lord, *"this would win a prize at the State Fair. Not first prize maybe, but certainly second. Tell you what, Peter. Send an angel down to hell with this leek. Let your mother grab hold, and the angel can pull her up."*

So Peter dispatches St. Michael with the leek. His armor gleams in the bowels of hell, but not half as splendidly as that marvelous leek. Finally, he find St. Peter's mother, who merely folds her arms across her chest and snaps, *"It's about time! Did that stupid son of mine finally talk sense into that Jew? When I think of all the meals I cooked for those twelve louts—"*

"No time to waste, Signora!" St. Michael says. *"Grab the head of this leek, and I'll pull you up!"* And St. Peter's mother latches onto the leek.

St. Michael flaps his mighty wings and begins the ascent. But as they slowly rise out of hell, the damned, including all the beggars St. Peter's mother turned away from her door, grab her skirts and hitch a ride. *"Give us some of that leek!"* they demand. *"We're still starving!"*

"No!" she shrieks. *"This is my leek! Mine! Get your own leek, you bums! My son's a saint!"*

She thrashes so violently to shake off the beggars that the tail of the leek snaps off, and St. Peter's mother tumbles to the bottom of hell. When St. Michael, with Peter present, informs the Lord what had happened, Christ frowns the way he does in that Byzantine mosaic in the cathedral of Monreale.

"Peter," he says, raising that bony finger, *"no more favors."*

The American owners—the Coltons and Crouses, Hoffmans and Ludlows, Thackaburys and Twogoods, Warrens and Wilsons— were nonplused by the imported feudalism. Whenever they inspected their property, the sharecroppers' houses and children were spick-and-span. If the Americans returned from church in a horse and buggy, the Sicilians lined the sidewalk in their best clothes and paid obeisance. That courtly bob of the head. *Padrun.* This devotion wasn't entirely staged or ironic. Whatever their faults, the American *padroni* were fair and generous, even building cabins near the mucklands to spare the sharecroppers the long walk. The Sicilians responded with affection and loyalty, cooking the Americans Old World delicacies, inviting them to weddings and baptisms, sometimes naming their children after them, forever grateful to those who had given them their first real opportunity in this new land.

But these immigrants were never naive. They saw how America worked and knew the stakes. If you lost in this country, you lost utterly. What other conclusion could be reached, when every Fourth of July the Oneida Indians passed through Main Street on a float like prisoners in a Roman triumph? Under a friendly sign, "CANASTOTA MEANS TREES BY STILL WATER," they wore imitation headgear and looked dejected. The Ku Klux Klan was active in Madison and Oneida counties, burning scarecrows of Italians and other undesirables in the fields, and when America joined World War I, the local toughs and Spanish-American War vets pressured some immigrants to enlist. The muddy trenches, they later joked, were almost as bad as the muck; but the tear gas wasn't as strong as the onions. They learned a mocking work song from the Brits:

> *Any complaints this morning?*
> *Do we complain? Not we!*
> *What's the matter with lumps of onion*
> *Floating around in the tea?*

Tempered by harsh experience, the Sicilians now saw the mucklands less poetically and more pragmatically. Within a decade, they had moved from feudalism to Jeffersonian agrarianism. As early as 1902, Michael Patterelli had bought five acres of land from Lucretia Thackabury in the Town of Lennox. Three years later, three other Italians—Libero Valerio, John Cerio, and Michael Bucci, grandfather of novelist Mary Bucci Bush—each bought ten to fifteen more acres. Over the next five years, ownership substantially increased, with a total of twenty-one immigrants owning 167 acres of land.

As a rule, holdings were small, on average no more than nine acres, often less. Money was limited, and the land took time to cultivate. To anchor the family financially, a husband or wife took a steady outside job at the Ideal Cut Glass or the Watson Wagon factory, while the remaining spouse and the children worked the land. Neighbors observed and learned from each other, creating a boom. By 1915, thirty-seven Sicilian families owned 341 acres. Over the next five years, the number of owners doubled while the amount of acreage tripled. By 1930 the Sicilians owned half the mucklands. After World War Two, they controlled ninety percent of it.

These onion farmers had never heard of, much less read, Virgil's *Georgics*, but one line in Book One could have been their motto: "*Labor omnia vincit improbus.*" Toil overcomes everything. And how they toiled! If picking onions had been running the gauntlet, operating an onion farm was the labors of Hercules. Before the actual planting in late April or early May, the land was ploughed, dragged, and fertilized. Although hand-operated machines could plant onion seeds in rows, more immediate results were obtained by planting sets, tiny dried onions, which were buried upland, where the hard ground discouraged their full growth before transplanting. True, machines were available to do this work, too, but they tended to dump the sets upside down, sideways, or too thickly; so most transplanting was done on hands and knees as the tender sets were placed in holes.

A hard row to hoe, but it was only the beginning. If the weather was good, the seedlings appeared above ground in a week, initiating a period of intensive weeding and cultivation. Again, machines could handle this job, but the best results were done by hand, another punishing ordeal. During the next months, the stalks dried up and fell off while the onions matured. The delicate work of topping onions, clipping off the dry tops, was usually done by children. Topping machines might damage or bruise the large bulbs. After harvest, the onions were cleaned, bagged, and sold at local markets or trucked to the village for storage. The more successful onion farmers owned warehouses and hoarded the crop till the price was right. Who the hell needs a middle man?

This collective enterprise gave the immigrant onion farmers financial, cultural, and political independence. Doris Lawson, the high-school English teacher who wrote a pamphlet on Canastota's Italians, deplored their pride and clannishness. Constituting a full third of the population, the Sicilians formed a village within the village, with their own neighborhoods, civic and recreational clubs, and church. Their parish was dedicated to my grandmother's namesake, St. Agatha, one of Sicily's three great protectors, the third-century Christian martyr whose breasts were torn by pincers. To shock their American neighbors, the Sicilians flaunted her rather explicit statue and served *minni di virgini,* pastries shaped like her severed breasts.

Despite this prickly independence, the immigrants weren't immune to environmental influence. Just as chives transformed Glaucus into a sea god, onions transformed these Sicilians into Americans. At first, the changes were subtle. According to Rose Raffa and Grace Tornatore, the curators of Canastota's Erie Canal Museum, the women led the way, subverting taboos one by one. They bought American baby bottles from Mr. Wilson the pharmacist, defying their husbands, who thought rubber nipples were unnatural. They ordered clothes from Sears Roebuck instead of settling for traditional black. They broke *omerta* by asking neighbors, "How do you get your wash so clean?" They went to the flicks on Sunday night, although custom dictated staying home. They bought Oneida silverware as a wedding gift, even when the pastor disapproved because the Oneida Community, the company founders, had practiced group marriage.

Not to be outdone, the men rebelled, too, but more flamboyantly. They built their own Fourth of July float, festooned with garlic and onions, and integrated American-style fireworks into the Feast of the Assumption, a traditional harvest festival. The finale was an explosive display called the Battle of the Marne, guaranteed to make the saints in heaven piss themselves. As if that weren't blasphemous enough, they also formed a union. Antonio G. Waldo, owner of Aching Back Farm on Onion Town Road, started the Canastota Growers Cooperative Association and headed both the New York State Vegetable Growers Association and the New York State Council for Farmer Cooperatives. The Klan burned him in effigy but couldn't stop him. During the forties, his cooperative represented the onion industry in New York City parades. Sponsored by a mouthwash company, they would march down Fifth Avenue with a banner: "EAT ONIONS—USE LISTERINE."

They had become Americans, at last.

BUT THE REAL AMERICANS were their children, who detested onion farming. For them, the muck was a curse, not a blessing.

During the summer, the consistency was like fine dust, and the slightest breeze filled the eyes and clogged the nostrils with black powder. When rain fell in spring and fall, it was like wallowing in manure. The Canastota kids came home so dirty that passers-by couldn't tell their color. Their schoolmates called them dinges. The old-timers told them to join a minstrel show. The taint was insufferable, and the miasma of your sweat, like the breeze from a wild onion patch, announced your presence five minutes before your arrival. Eddie Giambastiani, who used to top onions on his grandfather's New Boston Road farm, had to join the navy to wash away the stink and the grime. Eventually, he became an admiral.

The younger generation was like that, restless and ambitious. Buried alive under a mountain of onions, they were going crazy. They couldn't fathom their parents' obsession. They knew more uses for onions than Eskimos knew names for snow; and God forbid you broke the rules, which were as strict and elaborate as Mosaic law. Every onion, for example, had a specific culinary function. Chives, shallots, and scallions were used primarily as herbs and seasonings. Leeks enhanced sauces and thickened stock, but, because they are so mellow and meaty, they were often served as a side dish. Regular onions, because of their variety and versatility, performed double duty.

These kitchen commandments enslaved the girls, who, after picking onions all day, cooked them all night. The time and care it took to prepare a single leek! Because leeks are "blanched," that is, buried in earth to be kept pale, they require painstaking cleaning—first peeled and sliced, then swished and soaked in a bowl of cool water, finally squeezed and strained to remove the dirt. This could take as long as an hour, and all you got as a reward were dirty looks from your brothers. You cried from frustration and blamed the onions. The old ways chafed.

Take those noxious folk remedies. More orders, more onions! Rub onions in cuts to disinfect them. Eat raw onions to sweat out a cold. Soak sore feet and hands in salted water with boiled onions. The same method shrinks boils and cures warts. Smear onion juice under your eyelid to remove a sty. Apply fried onions to your chest to decongest the lungs. Shove a pearl onion up your ass to relieve piles. Years later, when American medicine prescribed onions to fight colds and cancer, some of these nostrums were validated. But for those coming of age in Canastota, they were guinea voodoo. How could you buy that used Chevy in Cazenovia if you wore an onion poultice?

Parents were unsympathetic and hectored their children to learn contentment. "Count your blessings!" they scolded. "It's a miracle you have what you have!" But the Canastota kids didn't see it that way. Blessings that fall like manna are a miracle. Blessings sustained by irk and sweat are an outrage. And no matter how often they tried to be grateful, no matter how many times they prayed or went to confession, they felt resentful. Worse, they didn't know whom to blame: God, for creating the world from onions, or their parents, for working like mules. So rage became their foster brother. He was at every family meal, even the most festive, sulking in the corner with a perpetual bowl of *pasta fazool*, glowering and shaking his head—a Caliban reeking of scallions. You ate with him, slept with him, and if you were lucky enough bathed with him, and this repeated contact lead to long internal debates. In the wee hours, the questions stung worse than the flies in the muck.

If you really were an American, why did you live on the north side of the tracks in a tumbledown house? Why did you spend every spare moment of your life in the muck, instead of joining track, singing in the chorus, or writing for the paper? Why did your varsity sweater always stink of the fields, no matter how often you washed it? Why did complete strangers have the right to call you filthy names, Onion Head, Guano Guinea, Mucker Fucker, and why did the teacher smirk when you mispronounced "The Lady of Shalott"? Why did your parents ignore these slights— pride, fatigue, ignorance? Why did they invest every penny in more farming equipment, whether or not that rusted tool shed could hold another John Deere tiller? Most of all, why did they force you to eat *pasta fazool* EVERY NIGHT, even when times were good; and why, when you objected, did they always quote the same galling proverb, "Meat is something that pulls a plough"?

John Dos Passos calls this process of self-examination "peeling the onion of doubt," and nobody could peel onions like the Canastota kids. The muck, they concluded, might be fine for their folks but not for them. They would bide their time and seek other opportunities. The young women planned to become secretaries, teachers, nurses, and librarians, while the more daring young men started their own businesses, even in the middle of the Depression. But ultimately the postwar boom allowed the majority to find long-term, profitable work beyond the onion fields. This was freedom, indeed, and a significant right of passage was spending one's first major paycheck.

Everyone fantasized about that big night on the town. And back then, a big night on the town meant going to Syracuse, where golden lights were strung across North Salina Street, the city's bustling shopping district, right in the heart of Little Italy, or to Utica, which was edgier, thanks to its Mafia mystique, and had fancier restaurants. Either way, the goal was to blow your entire wad. What else was it for? This was the first money that was truly yours, not simply fodder for the table or a cut from the farm. The real green, not some goddamn leek. But some Canastota kids would learn that, no matter how they had earned their money, it still smelled like onions.

This is what happened to everyone's favorite eager beaver, Charlie Borgononi. Even as a teen, Charlie, born Cesare, displayed the same drive and flair that would make him chaplain of the Syracuse University football and basketball teams and director of the Pompeii Players, America's most successful amateur musical theater company. To celebrate his first paycheck, Charlie invited his brothers to a tony meal at Grimaldi's, not the one on Syracuse's Erie Boulevard, mind you, but the original in Utica, a Tuscan villa of plaster festoons, Botticellian frescoes, and gilded mirrors. They sat around the table, four husky, ham-fisted guys with the same ferreting eyes and truculent grin. Their rented dinner jackets, barely wrinkled from the ride in that crowded Buick, fitted perfectly. They were no longer rubes from Onion Town but dashing men about town.

As the brothers admired the silverware and played with the mitered napkins, the waiter appeared, a diminutive, slick-haired man with the bobbing walk of a crow. Charlie conversed with him in Italian, which delighted the waiter, and his obsequious banter made Charlie more expansive. "Let's have the house special!" Charlie said. "Spare no expense!" And the waiter bowed and scraped. Charlie hadn't asked what the house special was, but the brothers preferred it that way. Not knowing was part of the fun.

The surprise would sweeten the anticipation, which had accompanied them for twenty hungry miles on Route 5. At last, something besides *pasta fazool!* What would it be? *Saltimbocca romano?* Chicken *piccante?* Clams *oreganato?* The maitre d' returned, beaming, carrying a large silver tureen. With a flourish, he uncovered it.

"*Pasta e fagioli!*" he announced.

The Borgononis glared at the bowl of beans, then at the waiter and clenched their fists. Murderously calm, Charlie motioned to the trembling waiter. "Is this a joke?" Charlie asked.

"N-no, Signore."

"You think we're a bunch of *cafons?*"

"It's the house special, Signore. I swear!"

"Well, take it away. Take it away," Charlie said, "and bring me a steak. A big fat juicy steak. Thick enough to choke a bear, *capisc'?* I want a steak so rare it moos when I poke it. And take this guinea food away!"

The waiter returned in five minutes with a steak, smothered in onions. He probably didn't mean to insult the Canastota boys, but Charlie overturned his chair and had to be restrained by his brothers. Sometimes I think he entered the priesthood just to keep from clobbering people.

CHARLIE'S NEIGHBOR, Carmen Basilio, had a better outlet for aggression—boxing. Since the days of the Erie Canal, when Irish workmen fought bare-knuckled in dockside rings, Canastota had been an important boxing center, but Carmen the Canastota Clouter would make his home town the site of the Boxing Hall of Fame. His fight with Sugar Ray Robinson for the middleweight championship of the world is arguably the greatest sporting event in Central New York history.

Carmen's father, Joseph Basilio, had emigrated from Rome, so maybe Carmen was destined to become a gladiator. Joe owned three patches of muck, the largest being thirty-two acres near Chittenango, where the family eventually settled. To manage his three eldest sons, Armando, Carmen, and Paul, he let them settle all arguments with boxing gloves. On Friday nights, they were allowed to stay up late and listen to radio broadcasts from Madison Square Garden. Carmen was partial to Joe Louis and Jimmy Braddock.

The boy was a paradox. He was the gentlest of Joe's sons, devoutly religious, obedient to a fault, a listener, not a talker, who loved solitary hikes, fishing, and rabbit hunting. The local Indians said he had a pure soul. "You'd have a hard time making a movie of him," said Oren Lyons, the Onondaga chief who became a close friend. "Carmen was so clean." But he was also a ferocious fighter. He boxed for Canastota High, later claiming he wouldn't have gone to school otherwise, and scuffled in the streets. God help the poor bastard who called him a wop. After serving in the Marines at the end of World War II and working on Joe's farm, the kid decided to turn pro.

Carmen began as a welterweight and submitted to a bruising apprenticeship. He suffered early and humiliating losses to medi-ocrities like Connie Ties and Mike Koballa. "Carmen got caramelized," people joked. He was booed in the ring and laughed at in the gym. Friends urged him to quit, but Carmen ignored them. He knew he had the right stuff. The onion fields had given him discipline and endurance, and the Marines had taught him technique. Gradually, he worked his way up and in 1953 defeated welterweight champion Billy Graham on television before becoming a middleweight. Over the next four years, he racked up 175 victories over the likes of Jake La Motta, Bobo Olsen, and Gene Fullner and competed for six titles in two weight categories.

Despite growing fame, Carmen continued working out in Syracuse's Little Italy, in the now-demolished Main Street Gym on the 300 block of North Salina. His rhythm and concentration were awesome. Nobody could work a speed ball better. According to one apocryphal anecdote, when an admirer asked Basilio the secret of his technique, Carmen replied, "I pretend it's an onion."

His big shot came when he was set to fight Sugar Ray Robin-son on September 23, 1957, in Yankee Stadium. Carmen had met Sugar Ray four years earlier, introducing himself as the guy who had beaten Billy Graham, but Sugar Ray brushed him off. Ever since, Carmen was resolved to fight him. Robinson thought Basilio was beneath him but agreed to the match for money. His take was forty-five percent of the gate, more than half a mil, while Basilio's was only twenty percent. Basilio greatly resented the inequity and couldn't stand Robinson's cockiness. Sugar Ray reveled in the high life and loved sounding off to reporters. At a press conference, he disparaged Italian fighters and said he wanted to visit Rome so he could stage a boxing demonstration for the Pope.

For Carmen, who knelt and prayed in the ring after every match, win or lose, this was the last straw. He trained with grim determination. On the Thursday before the Monday night bout, he shattered the jaw of sparring partner Archie Whitfield, a twenty-year-old middleweight from Chicago, without breaking his stride or apologizing. Sugar Ray had better watch out.

The fight was brutal; fifteen bloody rounds, toe-to-toe. Carmen's *paisani* watched the closed-circuit broadcast at the sold-out State Fair Coliseum. The early rounds were very close. Both men battered each other relentlessly. Each time Basilio carved out an advantage, Robinson rallied. For every bruising shot Robinson got off, Basilio bounced back with a flurry of punches. At one point, Sugar Ray gashed Carmen's left eye, which later required four stitches, but Carmen's superior stamina, the result of all those years working in the Canastota onion fields, turned the tide. By the eleventh round, Robinson was winded, and, seeing an advantage, Basilio pinned him against the ropes and hit him thirty-four straight times. That tipped the balance. When the bell rang, by a two-to-one decision, Carmen Basilio was the middleweight champion of the world.

Times Square, which was packed with Central New Yorkers, erupted, while upstate the headline of the *Syracuse Herald-Journal* blared, "ALL HAIL, CARMEN THE KING!" At the Syracuse train station, the champ was greeted by hundreds of fans, scores of Marines, friends from Canastota, Mayor Donald Mead, and the Schnitzelfritz band. Parades followed in Chittenango and Canastota. The triumph was short-lived. Just six months later, in a Chicago rematch, Basilio lost the title to Robinson and, despite two more efforts, never recaptured it. He left the ring, worked in the athletic department at Le Moyne College, and became a representative for Genesee Brewery. He lost the 1980 mayoral race in Chittenango by 66 votes.

CANASTOTA SEEMED TO FADE with its champion. By the late seventies, only two major onion farmers were still in business, Izzy

Rapasadi and Sam Giufre. Out of habit, they quoted shopworn Sicilian proverbs. "The eyes of the owner fattens the horse," Sam liked to say; that is, a closely watched business always prospers. But hardly anyone was left to listen. Most second-generation Canastotans had left the village, and their parents, realizing the mucklands had no future, had aided and abetted their flight. Whenever the kids would call from SUNY Oswego or Fort Drum, crying from homesickness, the response was always the same: "Come on back! The muck is waiting!" The dorm and the barracks seemed less daunting then.

Young Canastotans would succeed in a cleaner if more insipid world than their parents', repairing power lines for Niagara Mohawk, selling industrial air conditioners for Carrier, working on military contracts for Martin Marietta, but they never achieved the same pioneer independence. Whatever its limitations, the muck had been wholly theirs, and the folks—like the onions they grew—had been raw but free. When American tried to chew them up, they left a tang in its mouth. What freedom could their children and grandchildren know in the suburbs of Rome, Manlius, and Fayetteville, where onion breath was taboo at PTA meetings, where supermarkets never carried chives or shallots, where neighborhood associations complained if you grew leeks in your yard? Whenever they bought a ten-pound bag of onions at the farmer's market, they wept for the past.

"Tears are for passing things," said Virgil, and Canasatota is passing away. Between 1978 and 1998, the population dropped from 5,033 to 4,637 but has held at 4,400 since the 2000 census. Even so, the future is hardly bright. The closing of Griffiss Air Force Base in 1995 killed the local economy, which explains why Canastota took twenty years to repay HUD $365,000 for low-interest business and development loans issued in 1982. Two years later, Mayor Todd Rouse and the village trustees sought another $600,000 from the Governor's Office for Small Cities to renovate low-income housing along the Erie Canal. Scott Rapasadi, deputy mayor and chair of the International Boxing Hall of Fame Induction Weekend, will settle for replacing the sidewalks on Main and Peterboro streets.

Meanwhile, the old dagos keep disappearing. Carmen Basilio has retired to Rochester but sometimes shows up to sign autographs at Tully's in Syracuse. After surviving a sextuple bypass in 1997, the champ has slowly declined: down for the count, but not out. But Monsignor Charles Borgognoni died on July 19, 2007. Parkinson's had peeled away his memories, songs, and stories, one by one. Confined in his last years to the James Square Health and Rehabilitation Center, he would stare into space and mutter the words *pasta fazool*. Rose Raffa and Grace Tornatore, the village vestals, still run the Canastota Canal Town Museum but face a drought of volunteers. Operating hours are noon to three, Tuesday through Saturday, but only sporadically. The museum's hiccupping answering machine does not exactly encourage tourism.

As for Nonna Agata, the onion-peeling sibyl who haunts my kitchen, she died March 1, 1986, on the Matronalia, the ancient Roman holiday honoring matriarchs and blessing the planting of crops. She was ninety-six years old, and, until she took that tumble on the sidewalk, had been in good health. After the fall, she quickly disintegrated. Mamma was ill at the time, and my sister and I were away at college, so my family lacked the resources to care for Nonna. Instead, my aunts placed her in a Coney Island nursing home, where the nurses abused and ignored her. Whenever we visited, her room always smelled of fried onion rings, leftovers from the orderly's boardwalk lunch. Except for the immediate family, no one attended her wake or funeral. She had outlived her entire world.

At the time, I was too upset to cry, but Papa told me not to sweat it. "You'll have a whole lifetime to cry," he said. He was right. Grief requires husbandry. Joy springs up like an iris after a cloudburst, but sorrow must be cultivated like an onion in the muck of regret. Hard work, but the harvest never fails. As the Romans would say, "*Lacrimae rerum.*" Tears are in everything.

And people wonder why I cry in my kitchen.

SECONDO

Tripe alla Romana

A Load of Tripe

TRIPE ALLA ROMANA

WHEN PREPARING THIS DISH, adopt General Kutuzov's motto in *War and Peace:* "Time and patience." Tripe is the ultimate slow food. But you can cut corners without sacrificing quality by ordering processed tripe from a reputable butcher or offal plant.

Even so, prepare for a long haul. Use the time constructively. If you have put off doing the taxes or painting the bathroom, now is your chance.

INGREDIENTS

- 3 pounds processed honeycomb tripe
- 2 celery stalks
- 2 carrots
- 2 large onions
- 3 tablespoons extra virgin olive oil
- ¼ to ½ teaspoon red pepper flakes
- 2 bay leaves
- ½ to ⅔ cup dry Italian wine
- 1 24-ounce can peeled whole tomatoes
- ½ teaspoon sea salt
- ½ teaspoon black pepper
- ½ teaspoon paprika
- 3 teaspoons fresh mint
- 4 tablespoons Pecorino Romano cheese

DIRECTIONS

1. Place the tripe in a colander and rise under running cold water for 10 minutes. Remove any fat with a paring knife.
2. Bring large pot of water to a boil, add the tripe, and boil for an hour.
3. Drain tripe in colander and transfer to a cutting board. Slice into strips the size and shape of your

index finger. If the tripe slivers resemble your middle
finger, your guests will be scandalized.

4. Peel and mince celery, carrots, and onions.

5. Heat oil in large pot and add root vegetables, Season
   with red pepper flakes and stir until vegetables wilt.
   Add tripe and bay leaves and toss. Sauté until vegetables begin to brown.

6. Pour wine and boil until reduced (1 to 2 minutes).

7. Drain and chop canned tomatoes and add to tripe.
   Season with salt, pepper, and paprika.

8. Raise heat to high until stew boils. Then lower heat,
   cover pot, and simmer for 30 minutes.

9. Garnish tripe with mint and turn off heat. Remove
   and discard bay leaves. Sprinkle with Romano and let
   pot sit for 5 minutes. Serve with more cheese if
   desired.

The tripe's texture should be spongy but yielding. Like your heart
on prom night. But if the tripe turns rubbery, feed the mess to
your cat and order take-out.

Your guests will thank you. So will your lawyer.

A LOAD OF TRIPE

No priest ever explained to me the mystery of the Incarnation. A Brooklyn butcher named Carmine Vaccaro taught me my catechism instead. At the time, I lived in a sun-blistered tenement on Twelfth Avenue and Fifty-third Street, where Bensonhurst melts into Borough Park. Married at Regina Pacis on Sixty-fifth Street, my newlywed parents had decided to settle in the neighborhood. Our entire world was wedged between Fort Hamilton Parkway and New Utrecht Avenue, and yet these childhood years remain the most expansive of my life. Everything had a cosmic dimension, from the thundering el to the billowing laundry. When the immigrant poet Pascal D'Angelo first came to L'America, he was convinced every street corner hid a shrine, because all the signs read "Ave, Ave, Ave." "What a religious place this must be," he mused, "to express its devotion at every crossing!" Greenhorn or not, D'Angelo was right. Brooklyn in the late fifties and early sixties was the New Jerusalem, and every errand was a pilgrimage, none more so than shopping for meat.

Mamma visited the butcher's at least three times a week, partly to compensate for the shoebox-sized freezer in our General Electric fridge, partly to escape the stench of chicken fat and soiled diapers from our downstairs neighbors, the Peratroskis. Reb Peratroski, the burly landlord and super, was a Hasidic *mohel* who, to support his seven squalling children, moonlighted as a kosher butcher. When they first met, my parents had asked if his competing jobs presented any problems. Reb Peratroski shrugged philosophically. "Meat is meat," he said. "And besides, it's all a *mitzvah*." Papa laughed and nodded, but Mamma blushed winsomely. She was the neighborhood's reigning beauty. Five years after her wedding, her bridal portrait still adorned the show window of Massari's, Bensonhurst's most prestigious photo shop, and would remain enshrined for another five years, even after we had moved to the suburbs of Freehold, New Jersey. Smitten, Reb

Peratroski doted on Mamma, offering to circumcise her firstborn for nothing and occasionally presenting her with sliced tongue wrapped in wax paper. Jealous of these gallantries, the babushkaed and perpetually pregnant Mrs. Peratroski would glare whenever Mamma left for the *goyisha* butcher's; and if, God forbid, she returned home with sausages, Mrs. Peratroski would spit "*Trayf!*" and slam her door.

Mamma never allowed these encounters to spoil her outings. Shopping for meat was the highlight of her week. Some mothers liked to window-shop at Macy's; my mother, an overworked seamstress, liked to imagine the fancy cuts she could buy, if she weren't limited by a shipping clerk's meager salary. Back then, Brooklyn had almost as many Italian butcher shops as Catholic churches, so Mamma had her pick. For simple orders, she would dash to La Rosa's Meat Market, the local butcher on Fifty-fifth Street under the New Utrecht el. For a change of venue, she would visit Frank and Sal's Prime Meats, still standing on Cristoforo Columbo Boulevard, the heart of Italian Bensonhurst. But for the best cuts and the most variety, not to mention a fine pretext for visiting Nonna Agata on Eightieth Street, Mamma would return to her old neighborhood in Dyker Heights, to Priolla's on Thirteenth Avenue.

Bustling, crowded, and ornate, Priolla's was pure guinea Baroque, a flamboyant study in contrasts. Spotless display cases clashed with the blood-soaked sawdust, while a strong miasma of Old Spice after-shave failed to camouflage the pervasive smell of offal. On the wall, an anatomized map of Italy complemented an atlas-sized meat chart; on the counter, a framed Sacred Heart stood beside an autographed picture of Ernest Borgnine as Marty: "*To the Priolla brothers,*" read the inscription, "*a cut above the rest!*"

The Priollas served a mostly Sicilian clientele. Raised in Catania, Sicily's enterprising Second City, they were born hucksters and formed a perfect team. Affable and cleft-chinned Johnny, the Adonis of Thirteenth Avenue, handled the deliveries; brainy and soft-spoken Vinny supervised the accounts, produced the circulars, and later drifted into advertising; but bossy and beefy Paulie punched the cash register and worked the scales. When he sharpened and flourished his knives, he could be as intimidating as Toscanini warming up the NBC Symphony, so few customers besides my mother contradicted him. For all that, he ran a jolly shop. As the neighborhood's most eligible bachelors and the local business association's live wires, the Priollas flirted with the prettiest girls and clowned behind the counter. Their outrageous horseplay crossed the zany anarchy of the Marx Brothers with the ritualized kabuki of Benihana. During Lent, for example, the Pirollas tenderized meat while chanting the liturgy:

> *Stabat Mater dolorosa*
> (Thump! thump! thump! thump!)
> *Iuxtra Crocem lacrimosa*
> (Thump! thump! thump! thump!)
> *Dum pendebat Filius*
> (Bang!)

This bit scandalized the more pious matrons, but it made perfect sense to me. After all, wasn't Christ the Lamb of God, and didn't we eat lamb for Easter, preferably with rosemary? And how the Priollas treated a slab of meat was nothing compared to how the Roman soldiers had treated our Savior. On the life-sized crucifix outside Santa Rosalia, our parish on Sixty-third Street and Fourteenth Avenue, Jesus hung like a side of beef. But the Priollas weren't being profound. They were hazing their junior butcher, Carmine Vaccaro.

An ex-seminarian and a part-time martyr, Carmine operated Priolla's Bone Yard, a refrigerated glass case packed with spongy sweat breads and glistening kidneys, coral-pink calf brains and bleeding hearts. Shy but intense, with an ascetic, melancholy face El Greco could have painted, he must have suffered from thyroid problems. His eyes bulged, and he habitually sucked coarse butcher's salt. After bolting from St. Joseph's Seminary in Yonkers, Carmine still attended daily mass and recited novenas to St. Luigi Gonzaga; but he considered Cardinal Francis Spellman, who had dedicated St. Joseph's recreation center, a glorified Rotarian. Well, at least he had eaten well. "*Chi se vo' impara' a magna', da li preti bisogna che va,*" Carmine once claimed, quoting a Roman proverb: If you wanna learn how to eat, you gotta go to the priests. To which Paulie retorted: "*'U Spiritu Santu nun abbotta.*" The Holy Spirit don't fill your belly.

Despite this ribbing, Paulie valued Carmine. His father, uncles, cousins, and grandfathers had worked in the Mattatoio, the great slaughterhouse of Rome's Testaccio district, so Carmine possessed an encyclopedic knowledge of organ meats. Nobody else knew more recipes for ox tail and knuckle bone or more ways to salvage week-old liver. His kindness and tact won the hearts of poor pensioners and struggling young housewives. Even when coated with gore, his hands were as delicate as a jeweler's.

"What'll it be, Mrs. D?" he asked one day.

"*Trippa!*" Mamma announced.

"Trip?" I said. "We goin' somewhere?"

The other customers laughed. From the case, Carmine removed something about the size, shape, and texture of a deflated soccer ball and placed it on the scale. When the gelatinous mass quivered, I grimaced. "Cow guts," Carmine explained.

Smiling bleakly, he slit open the bladder with a small paring knife and motioned me closer. The insides smelled worse than old sneakers but were as delicately brocaded as Mamma's wedding dress. Carmine invited me to stroke it. "See?" he said. "That's all we are, kid. That's all God is. We're born between piss and shit."

Later, when I learned Latin in Christian Brothers Academy, I would realize he had quoted St. Augustine: "*Inter faeces et urinam nascimur.*" We are born between feces and urine, and yet with an immortal soul. But for now, I was struck by the awe and irony in his voice. What *was* this stuff? I wondered.

"Go peddle your tripe!" growled Paulie.

TRIPE COMES FROM the stomach lining of any ruminant, but beef tripe is the most common. Like all ruminants, cows must digest their food in two stages. That doesn't mean their digestive system is more primitive than that of other mammals; on the contrary, it is ingeniously designed to extract the most nutrients from vitamin-deficient leaves and grass. To accomplish this vital task, cows employ four stomach chambers: the *rumen*, the *reticulum*, the *omasum*, and the *abomasum*.

The first two chambers partially digest food. The pocket-like rumen mixes raw material with bile, using symbiotic bacteria to convert cellulose into glucose, while the muscular reticulum mashes and kneads the half-digested mess into a wad of cud, formally called the *bolus*. The cow regurgitates the cud, slowly chews and mixes it with more bile to break down the remaining fibers, then re-swallows the lump, which passes to the last two stomach chambers.

After the omasum extracts all moisture, the abomasum sends the digested food to the small intestine, where the final absorption of the nutrients occurs. Interestingly, almost all the glucose extracted from the cellulose feeds the cow's symbiotic bacteria. The cow itself takes its energy from the volatile fatty acids produced by its parasitic tenants: acetic acid, propionic acid, and butyric acid. The entire process can take up to fourteen hours; and because ruminants look so thoughtful while chewing their cud, we have the word *ruminate.*

Of a cow's four stomachs, only the first three are sold in Italian butcher shops. Each has a colorful nickname. Rumen tripe is *La Tasca* or *Il Beretto* because it can look like a pocket or a cap. Omasum tripe, resembling the leaves of an ancient family Bible, is *La Bibbia.* But reticulum or honeycomb tripe—the most prized because it is the meatiest and tenderest of the three—is called *La Francesi,* the French Woman. *Reticulum,* the Latin for reticle or net, is the root word for reticule: a woman's mesh drawstring handbag, popular in the eighteenth and nineteenth centuries. *La Francesi,* Carmine used to say, sometimes leaves a tip in her purse. Occasionally, if you cut open unprocessed honeycomb tripe, you will find a nail, a coin, a bit of wire, even a St. Anthony's medal. Some cows suffer from Hardware Syndrome and will eat almost anything. Fortunately, the safety net of the reticulum often prevents disembowelment, not to mention spikes the mineral content of an Italian family meal.

"No matter how it's cooked," declared the nineteenth-century gourmet Pelligrino Artusi, "tripe is an ordinary dish." It should never be eaten by the dyspeptic or the gouty, he averred, unless prepared in the proper Tuscan way; an unnecessary bit of chauvinism. A rich silk merchant, who had retired early to devote himself to high cuisine, Artusi considered tripe fit only for private family meals, and even then only in working-class homes. Nevertheless, this model of rectitude secreted Florence's dingiest tripe shops the way Gladstone missionized Whitechapel brothels. The Maestro convinced himself this slumming was to secure tripe broth for his sophisticated risottos, but he always returned home with ten kilos of tripe, much to his children's delight.

Tripe is an ambivalent soul food. A delectable and disgusting tangle of guts, it provokes spleen and triggers intestine warfare. If you want to see Italians quarrel, don't ask them about the Church, the Mafia, or Mussolini; ask them about tripe. Everyone has an opinion. Chefs insist this dish is for heroes and kings. In Homer's *Iliad*, Agamemnon's cooks mollify the surly Achilles with a bowl of tripe. During the eleventh century, William the Conqueror so loved *Tripes à la Caen* that when Phillip I, the bloated and sarcastic King of France, disparaged the dish, William vowed he would "come and be churched at Notre Dame de Paris with ten thousand lances instead of candles." Incidents like this make physicians shake their head. Tripe, they maintain, can be fatal. According to Dr. Francois Rabelais, Gargamelle gave birth to Gargantua after eating a huge dish of *godebillios*, the succulent tripe of oxen fattened on rich *guimo* meadows. The convulsive labor pains killed her. Likewise, waggish historians claim, the birth of Italy was fated to produce the same tragic *agita*, because so many revolutionaries patronized Genoa's Antica Tripperia, Italy's oldest tripe shop.

If you visit this *trattoria* today, still standing in the *centro storico* at the mouth of the narrow Vico della Casana near Piazza Soziglia, you will see the same large copper saucer pans and white marble bar that served Verdi and Mazzini, Garibaldi and D'Azeglio. As they chewed the fat, or rather, the gristle, these Romantics and idealists believed they could unite Italy, even as they squabbled over which of the country's twenty feuding regions had the best tripe dish. In Treviso, they serve it with parsley and chicken stock; in Turin, with wild mushrooms; in Genoa, with beans, peas, and potatoes; in Milan, with butter, asparagus, and rice; in Lucca, with cinnamon and cloves; in Florence, with green sauce and grilled peppers; in Naples, plain with salt and lemon juice; in Palermo, deep-fried and stuffed in a salted bun. But the archetypal tripe dish, most Italians will concede, remains *trippa alla romana*, and that means visiting the Testaccio, Carmine Vaccaro's ancestral neighborhood, and sampling its gusty *Quinto-Quarto* cuisine.

ROME'S *RIONI*, its traditional districts, come from the fourteen Latin *regiones* into which Augustus divided the Eternal City. Over the past two millennia, their number and size have changed, with combinations and redistricting dictated by crisis, expediency, and sheer graft. Although the present subdivisions were made in 1921, the district coats of arms date back to 1744 and are displayed on prominent street corners, usually next to old wall plaques detailing obsolete administrative orders. Of today's twenty-two *rioni*, nineteen are on the east bank of the Tiber, while three are on the west bank. The Testaccio, a former working-class stronghold, is the capital's southern district. Small and compact, the neighborhood is bound to the west and south by the Tiber and to the north by the elegant Aventine Hill. Across the river are the rival Trastevere district and the ancient Jewish ghetto. To the east are the World War II British military cemetery and the nineteenth-century Protestant *campo santo* containing the remains of Keats's lungs and Shelley's heart.

Once located outside the city walls, the neighborhood takes its name ("Nogginville") from a skull-shaped hill of amphora shards called Monte Testaccio, a haphazard monument to classical Rome's fluvial trade. From the fifth century B.C. until the fall of the empire, oil and wine arrived at the Tiber's southern port in terra-cotta amphorae, narrow-necked, two-handled jars resembling human heads. The Romans nicknamed these containers *testae,* the possible origin of the insult "jughead." Since the city magistrates were a no-deposit, no-return bunch, they issued hammers and assigned thousands of slaves to smash each arriving terra-cotta jar and stack the fragments in a designated section within the Aurelian Wall. After eight centuries, the pieces formed *Mons Testaceus,* a weed-choked mound 160 feet tall and a quarter mile around.

Besides functioning as an imperial garbage dump, the Testaccio used to be Rome's primary shambles and stockyard. Up until the late 1960s, in fact, cattle freely roamed the outskirts of the Eternal City, and fittingly so. After all, Rome's Seven Hills began as prime grazing land. According to myth, Hercules rescued his prize herd from Caucus, a cattle-rustling giant, on the Palantine. Romulus and Remus, who spent their fugitive early years disguised as cowboys, tended the flock of their foster father, Faustulus, on the Aventine. These legends sound bucolic, but the reality was grim and sordid. Drudgery degraded and stupefied man and beast. Recall the heartbreaking passage in Book Three of Virgil's *Georgics,* where feeble cattle, wreathed and filleted, are too tired to feel the sacrificial blade. They almost welcome being butchered. A more fitting end, Virgil sighs, than dropping dead of exhaustion in the fields. Steaming under the plough's strain, an ox collapses, puking blood and foam, and groans its last breath in the very furrow it has created. Sadly, the ploughman unyokes the mate that mourns its brother and leaves the plough stuck there, its work unfinished. So much for Arcadia.

The Industrial Revolution, not pastoralism, created the modern Testaccio. During the early nineteenth century, wooden shacks had mushroomed at the city's southern edge. Herdsmen and their families had moved closer to the city to supplement their household incomes. The more independent established makeshift butcher shops, while the young tried their luck in the new factories. Exploiting this unusual labor, clever capitalists converted bankrupt distilleries into tripe processing plants. Since the overhead was low, the risk was minimal. These facilities, however, must have stunk like the Devil's anus, judging from a bitter protest lodged in 1860, which compared tripe fumes to malaria. Undeterred, the plant owners dispatched pushcarts to promote their wares. Called *tripparoli,* these street peddlers went from house to house crying, "Tripe, trotters, and the rest of the muzzle!" They often carried a *schifo,* a skiff-shaped tray laden with tripe, pig's feet, and calf heads. That is how *schifo* became Italian slang for disgusting, and why Italian Americans call a repulsive person a skeeve. By the mid–nineteenth century, tripe had become so common that the dialect poet Giuseppe Belli used it as a metaphor for the human condition: "*Er monno é una trippetta, e l'omo é un gatto/Che je tocca aspettà la su'porzione.*" The world is a load of tripe, and man is a cat who must await his portion. Taking the hint, Ernesto Nathan, perhaps Rome's greatest mayor, created a tripe fund for stray cats, an incentive to rid the Campidoglio of rats.

The engine that finally transformed the Testaccio from a shanty town into an urban neighborhood, however, was the Mattatoio, Rome's colossal slaughterhouse built in 1890. Consisting of two huge pavilions, the 105,000-square-meter facility still stands beside the Lungotevere Testaccio, which skirts the Tiber, and the derelict Foro Boario. Now a cultural center operated by MACRO,

the Museum of Contemporary Roman Art, the Mattatoio pro-
claimed the capitalist ethos of Italy's dawning Belle Èpoque. Engineer Gioacchino Ersoch, architect emeritus of the City of Rome,
wanted to depict the transition from classicism to modernity, to
match the monumentality and rationale of turn-of-the-century
British and American industrial design without sacrificing Italian
nationalism.

While the slaughterhouse's interior foreshadowed the Ford
Rouge plant in Dearborn, Michigan, its exterior resembled a
Roman temple, complete with a marble pediment and pilaster.
Chiseled over the entrance are these words: "STABILMENTE DI MAT-
TAZIONE." A grandiloquent way of saying "shambles." Dr. Johnson
would have gnashed his teeth. One can only imagine his reaction
to the pagan statuary. A muscular cherub wrestles to the ground a
curve-horned steer, an allusion to Mithra's slaying the sacred bull.
When the Persian sun god's cult flourished on the Seven Hills,
priests would sprinkle the faithful with bull's blood. Likewise, the
peasants who submitted themselves to the Mattatoio's bloody bap-
tism were reborn as Rome's proletariat.

Most were grateful. Despite often brutal conditions, the factory offered steady work. At its zenith, the Mattatoio employed
thousands of *vaccinari*—cowhands, skinners and butchers who
came to live nearby. As part of their pay or as an occasional bonus,
these humble workers received portions of the cattle's *quinto
quarto,* or fifth quarter. Roman butchers would "quarter" cattle
into various valuable cuts; the fifth quarter is an elegant euphe-
mism for entrails and Cinderella meats: ears, cheeks, dewlaps, testicles, hocks, hoofs. By recuperating every edible part of a carcass,
these butchers observed not only economic thrift but religious
scruple. Mindful they worked in the shadow of the *Cupolone,* that
is, the great dome of St. Peter, they knew their secret duty was
feeding the poor, who rarely ate meat more than once a week. If
God Himself did not stint when sacrificing his only Son, neither
would they. This reverent practice created the Testaccio's unique
cuisine, in which liver, heart, tripe, tongue, intestine, glands, and
oxtails are turned into appetizing dishes, out of sheer necessity or
daredevil inspiration. Mrs. Peratrowski, my former landlady,
would have called such fare "*goyisha essen.*" *Quinto-Quarto* cooking
definitely smacks of the desperate and blasphemous, but that

should be expected. Rome's poor, after all, claim descent from the wolfish Remus, who profaned the rites of Pan by gobbling a sacrificial goat's hissing entrails as they roasted on the altar.

By the time the Mattatoio closed in 1975, small, family-run *trattorias* specializing in fifth-quarter dishes had sprouted all over the Testaccio. The oldest, largest, and best of these is Checchino, built right into the hill and across from the slaughterhouse. Founded in 1887, the establishment has been owned and operated for five generations by the Mariani family, the creators of Rome's beloved *coda alla vaccinara,* oxtail stew with tomato sauce and celery. Cooled to a constant 53–57 degrees Fahrenheit by Monte Testaccio's terra cotta shards, the restaurant's labyrinthine wine cellar contains over forty thousand bottles, including the Vatican's most prized vintage. The menu is equally impressive. Here you may feast on *rigatoni con la pajata* (rigatoni with milky veal intestines); *animelle* (sautéed sweetbreads); *schienale* (delicate veal or lamb spinal marrow); *coratella coi carciofi* (lamb heart, lung, and liver stew with artichokes); *testina di vitello prezzolinata* (veal cheeks in a parsley sauce); and of course *trippa alla romana.*

Smothered in tomato sauce, sprinkled with pecorino cheese, and garnished with wild spearmint from Ostia Antica, Checchino's tripe popularized the quarter. At first, the restaurant drew students, artists, and theater people; then, as the neighborhood grew trendier, came the journalists, politicians, movie stars, and intellectuals. Naturally, the clergy raided the Vatican cellar, without necessarily replenishing its stock. ("Haven't these guys ever heard of the Marriage at Cana?" the wine steward once grumbled.) Such a cross-section of Roman society inevitably generates the most Rabelaisian table talk. *We all shit what we eat,* the locals like to say, *but some shit we won't eat.*

When it comes to the Testaccio's raunchier delicacies, where do gluttonous Romans draw the line? Some will turn down fried chicken blood. Others will pass on tomato sauce with cock's crests, marinated beef spleen, pan-fried bull testicles, breaded pig vulvas, or boiled lamb head. But almost everyone loves tripe because it passes so trippingly on the tongue. Maybe that explains why Checchino regulars love to speechify. An impressive, if apocryphal, example of this extemporaneous art is Cardinal Fiorenzo Angelini's tripe sermon.

One Corpus Christi, Cardinal Angelini supposedly visited the Testaccio to celebrate the tenth anniversary of his secretary's ordination. One of the college's oldest and most venerable cardinals, Angelini has spent his entire life in Rome. No longer eligible for papal election, he has shunned power and has concentrated instead on hospital ministry, for which he earned a red hat and the irreverent nickname *Cardinale Padella,* Cardinal Bedpan. Even so, this true Prince of the Church is much beloved, despite a soft spot for Pius XII that makes some admirers wince. The hostess knelt and kissed his ring, and the waiters fussed. But when the Croatian bus boy offered to bring a screen for the cardinal's dinner party, His Eminence waived it away. "We should be among the people," he said. The maitre d', a hard-bitten Communist, nodded and grunted his approval: "*Servitor servorum Dei.*" Servant to the servants of God.

As dinner was served, the cardinal ate his *trippa alla romana* with gusto, while the secretary sullenly picked at his food. When the cardinal noticed, the shamefaced young priest confessed he had succumbed to the sin of pride, for he had considered it undignified for His Eminence to eat tripe like a common laborer. Angelini kindly smiled and swirled his Frascati. Rather than reprove the secretary, the cardinal invited him to practice exegesis. As with sacred scripture, he explained, diners should not limit themselves to tripe's literal meaning; they also should seek its moral, allegorical, anagogical meaning.

Might we not, for example, consider tripe a symbol of the human soul? After all, the Church teaches that the soul embraces our corporeal and spiritual totality. Thomas Aquinas, in fact, calls the soul "the form of the body," the vital power animating, pervading, and shaping up from conception to death. (Very Aristotelian, but then the Angelic Doctor was as fat as an ox.) And what of Maximus the Confessor, who compared the soul to a membrane, the boundary between heaven and earth, the material and spiritual, much like tripe stands between digestion and excretion? Foraging on creation, the incarnated soul ingests sensation and experience, converts them to thought and desire, and nourishes both natural talent and supernatural longing.

"But what does it shit, *Eminenza?*" an eavesdropping toddler asked.

"Theology," said the maitre d', and the restaurant exploded with laughter.

BROOKLYN IS AN OCEAN away from Rome, and specialty meats easily spoil. By the time my family moved to New Jersey, the tripe trade nearly had vanished. Pushcarts rarely visited the Italian neighborhoods, and when they did, the operators tended to be black World War II vets, who had served in Italy, or young Puerto Ricans hawking *menudo*. If I wanted to see an Italian tripe peddler, I had to wait till Christmas, when the old timers in Dyker Heights assembled their marvelous *presepios*. No self-respecting Nativity scene would be complete without a *trippaio*'s or tripe vendor's stall decorated with its garland of terracotta lemons. Needless to say, Freehold's spotless, fluorescent-lit Shop Rite didn't stock tripe. When we asked, the meat department manager bristled and shamed us.

Exiled in white-bread suburbia, I pined for *trippa romana*. Like a transatlantic umbilical cord, its memory connected me to Rome's nurturing matrix. Even when tripe wasn't in my mouth, it remained on my lips, for I continued to use tripe-based Italian idioms long after I had learned English. If a grudging matron short-changed me a candied apple for Halloween, I would call her a *trippalunga*, a slab of tripe; that is, a mean-hearted skinflint. If a schoolyard deadbeat asked to borrow more milk money, I would flick my chin and say: "*Nun c'è ttrippa pe' ggatti.*" (Literally, "There's no tripe for cats.") This handy expression means: "No fucking way. You're imposing on me," much like a cat begging giblets from a butcher. But with formal education and a scholarly career, these tangy idioms disappeared from my speech, casualties of assimilation. Academia is no place for soul food. I doubt Cornell West or Henry Louis Gates still eat chitlins; but if they do, their teaching schedules certainly prevent them from preparing it.

Tripe is equally time-consuming. Starting a full day in advance of cooking, you must mix one cup of kosher salt and one cup of vinegar, pour a third of the mixture into a large bowl and add the tripe, scrub the tripe vigorously with a brush, rinse the tripe under cold running water, then repeat the process two more times. Next, you transfer the tripe to a bowl, drown it in cold water, and cover and chill it in the refrigerator between eight and sixteen hours, changing the water once about halfway through. Then you place the tripe in a large stock pot with abundant water and a cup of white wine, throw in an onion, a carrot, a celery stalk, and some parsley, bring to a boil, reduce to a simmer, and cook the tripe for four to five hours, skimming the scum that often rises to the surface. When finally tender, the tripe can be cut into finger-wide strips and stewed to your liking; that is, if you have an extra two hours to spare.

Not surprisingly, given such constraints, I have cooked tripe only once in the past forty years. This attempt—a SAD-induced, twenty-eight-hour cooking marathon in the middle of a blizzard—ended disastrously. The result resembled hot-water-bottle bouillabaisse. Nevertheless, I ate every rubbery bite and afterwards felt oddly better. The real pain came when I related this incident to my colleagues, Cornell-educated WASPs. Quietly repulsed, they shunned me for a week, avoiding eye contact in the hall or smiling tightly in the copy room. Finally, I confronted them. "Look," I said, "you've no right to be squeamish! God knows the tripe you people eat! Marxist theory, Kundalini yoga! At least mine's the real thing!"

This outburst amused my colleagues, who restored me to the academic fold, but Ernest Hemingway, who loved fried tripe with mustard sauce, might have agreed. After witnessing the butchery of Caporetto, Hemingway concluded that abstract words like religion, art, and democracy are obscene. The only decent words are the names of rivers and villages. Everything else is offal from the Chicago stockyards. But we always forget. Famished for meaning, dignity, love, greedy humans will swallow whatever scraps church and state toss. We are gluttons for punishment. To quote a Romans proverb: "*Er gargarozzo é'stretto, ma cce cape la casa co'tutt'er tetto.*" The throat may be narrow, but if you chew and chomp, you can get down a whole house, including the roof. Confronted by animal necessity, the poor embrace a truth even the saints evade, that serenity has less to do with transcendental faith than with intestinal fortitude. With enough time and garnish, anything will pass.

None of this philosophy, mind you, satisfies my perpetual craving for tripe, or for a boon companion with whom to share it. "Who will join me in a dish of tripe?" invites Günter Grass. "It soothes, appeases the anger of the outraged, stills the fear of death, and reminds us of former days, when a half-filled pot of tripe was always on the stove." I always could visit Babbo down in the Village, I suppose, but that means a five-hour bus ride from Ithaca, New York. And besides, what self-respecting Brooklyn kid will shell out thirty bucks for a bowl of cow guts when he can pay fifty cents a pound at his neighborhood Tops? I owe it to Carmine Vaccaro to do the right thing.

CONTORNO

*Apulian Broccoli
Rabe Salad*

Bitter Greens

APULIAN BROCCOLI RABE SALAD

THIS EARLY SPRING SALAD defeats the winter blues. Like dandelion, broccoli rabe purifies the liver and cleanses the bowels; but to please the tongue, choose only the youngest greens.

For a briny contrast between the bitterness of the rappi and the bite of the red pepper, add a cup of pitted and chopped Kalamata olives or a half dozen mashed anchovy fillets.

INGREDIENTS
- 1 pound broccoli rabe, washed, trimmed, and cut into 3-inch pieces
- Sea salt
- 2 to 3 minced garlic cloves
- 7 tablespoons freshly squeezed lemon juice
- 7 tablespoons extra virgin olive oil
- Freshly ground pepper
- ½ teaspoon red pepper flakes
- 1 medium red onion or 3 shallots, chopped

DIRECTIONS
1. Place rappi in colander, bring large pot of water to boil, and immerse greens until the thickest stems are cooked but firm (2 to 3 minutes). If you prefer, steam the greens.
2. Drain and rinse under cold water and dry in salad spinner.
3. Combine the garlic, lemon juice, olive oil, salt, and red pepper flakes in a medium-sized bowl and blend with a whisk.
4. Add blanched rappi and chopped onions or shallots. Toss, cool at room temperature for 15 minutes, and serve.

During summer, this side dish can be converted into a main course. Poach 8 ounces of calamari in the leftover hot water, cut into ¼-inch thick rings, and add to salad before dressing and tossing.

But don't overcook the calamari! If you do, you might as well use the squid rings for washers the next time you fix the faucet.

BITTER GREENS

"DEFEAT ISN'T BITTER, if you don't swallow," Mamma said. She trimmed, chopped, and sautéed two bunches of Andy Boy broccoli rabe while I moped at the headlines. New York governor Mario Cuomo, the son of an immigrant grocer, had withdrawn from the 1988 primary. Ever since the last Democratic convention, where his eloquent keynote about America's two cities—one rich, one poor—had rebuked the greed and arrogance of the Reagan era, I had pictured him as president. Now George Herbert Walker Bush, the Connecticut blueblood who had never seen a supermarket scanner, would waltz into the Oval Office and ban broccoli from the White House menu.

I crumpled the paper and turned to Mamma.

"Sounds like a proverb. Sicilian?" I asked.

Mamma shook her head and stirred the greens. The battered, antique iron skillet could have been rescued from the wreck of an ancient galleon. "Sardinian," she said. "Compared to Sardinians, Sicilians are Pollyannas."

I nodded grimly. Even the honey is bitter in Sardinia, Cicero claimed. When the Romans colonized the island during the First Punic War, the natives showed indomitable contempt. Rather than greet their conquerors with cheers and garlands, as the Romans expected, they lined the streets of Cagliari and bitterly smiled at the passing war chariot. The silence was more oppressive than the heat.

To make amends, the city consul invited the Roman general, Titus Manlius Torquatus, to a peace banquet. A member of an old and distinguished patrician family, Torquatus claimed that Roman bondage surpassed barbarian freedom. The city fathers said nothing; but when slaves presented a tray of suspicious-looking vegetables, the general stopped boasting. He had heard about Sardinian hospitality. Often the islanders poisoned their enemies by serving a local weed containing a strychnine-like alkaloid. Victims convulsed, wracked by spasms of blood-spattering laughter, and died with a hideous grin—the infamous *risus sardonicus,* a Sardinian or sardonic smile. Torquatus politely declined the side dish and asked for *rapum,* fried bitter greens. This humble request appeased the Sardinians and probably saved the general's life.

Mamma heaped the steaming broccoli rabe on a large platter and set it before me. Leaning over, she whispered a riddle in my ear: "What makes bitter things sweet?"

"Hunger!" I replied.

She kissed my cheek and cut three thick slices of semolina bread. Using the *New York Times* as a tablecloth, I twirled the rabe on a fork, mashed and spread it on the sesame-seeded bread, and stuffed the hunk into my mouth. The olive oil dripped onto the newspaper and stained the Cuomo article: "*The decision I've made I think is best for my state, best for my family and, I think also, best for my party.*" Whatever you say, Mario. But disappointment already was dissolving into contentment, thanks to rabe's alchemy.

Mamma apologized for not adding sausage, but the greens, I assured between bites, were perfect. The coarse sea salt, crushed garlic cloves, and hot pepper flakes made their sharp bitterness sublime. Mamma wiped my grateful tears with her apron.

"God, I love bitter greens!" I cried.

"You'd better," Mamma said. "Sometimes that's all life puts on our plate."

BROCCOLI RABE IS Italian soul food, guinea collards. Since classical times, this bitter green has sustained and defined the dispossessed of the Mezzogiorno. But for Americans raised on steamed broccoli and triumphalism, broccoli rabe is swamp weed. Whenever I serve it as a *contorno* or side dish, white-bread dinner guests blink, stare, or grimace. The more polite will chew and smile, until my attention is distracted, and then spit the pulpy mess into a napkin. Bland food feeds complacency; but a bitter taste, like a bitter emotion, requires painful reconciliation.

"No matter how skillfully a cook mitigates and complements a bitter ingredient," explains *New York Times* food critic Molly O'Neill, "the pleasure that is obtained depends on one's ability to forgive. And so it is with broccoli rabe—still regarded with suspicion here in America." Indeed, political commentators who joked about the so-called Arugula Gap during Barack Obama's bid for the White House would have been better off discussing the nation's Rabe Gap.

Once forage for Italian immigrants sold at 25¢ a pound, now a gentrified delicacy for yuppies priced at $4.50 a bunch, broccoli rabe is more expensive and exotic than its common cousins: broccoli, cabbage, and kale. For this reason, most meat-and-potatoes Red Staters consider rabe elitist and hate it on principle. Its bitterness outrages Main Street, just as its etymology and taxonomy shock the Linguistic Society of America and baffle the Smithsonian Botanical Department. All attempts to assimilate it have failed. Despite the missionary efforts of gourmet magazines, not to mention crackdowns from the Departments of Agriculture, Immigration and Customs, and Homeland Security, broccoli rabe remains incorrigibly un-American—a symbol of poverty and exploitation.

That's why Italian Americans eat it. Like *maror* at a Passover Seder, broccoli rabe reminds us about bondage and oppression amidst freedom and affluence. This weed of exile and exploitation, this crucifer that flaunts rather than bears its cross, undermines America's Thanksgiving Day fantasies about the past. Its reproachful taste makes the most delectable lie impossible to swallow. As Sandra M. Gilbert suggests, broccoli rabe represents "the alienating taste of loss that accompanies cultural displacement, the mouthful of bitter herbs that immigrants swallow as they journey from the known to the unfathomable, from the table of the familiar to the walls of estrangement."

LIKE MOST FUGITIVES, broccoli rabe goes by many names: *brocoletto, brocoletti di rabe, broccoli de rabe, cime de rapa, raab, rapa, rapine, rapini, rappi, rappone*. Such aliases make middle-class Americans anxious. When seeking this shady green, even sophisticated shoppers in a college town like Ithaca, New York, will balk, as if forced to give a password in a mob joint. At the local Wegmans, I once saw a statuesque Cornell Heights matron in a salt-and-pepper Angelheart tunic approach the produce manager with trepidation. It took her five whole minutes to work up the courage to ask:

"Do you have any broccoli rape?"

Immediately, she realized her mistake and turned redder than the beets being washed by a gaping stocker. The produce manager stiffened with wounded dignity.

"Lady," he replied, "our vegetables behave themselves."

Actually, the word *rabe* derives from *rapum,* the Latin for turnip. Pliny the Elder considered the turnip the most important vegetable in the Roman diet after cereal and beans, "since its utility surpasses that of any other plant." His *Natural History* lists twelve distinct types of *rapum.* Before the spread of potatoes, this highly nutritive root vegetable was among the most important staples for man and beast. Excellent fodder, turnips grow in even the poorest soil. Roman farmers valued the turnip's utility. If left in the ground till next harvest, it replenishes the soil and prevents famine. But Roman cooks admired the turnip's versatility. The bulbous taproot works well in a soup or stew, while the leafy greens can be prepared as a salad or side dish.

Rapum was associated with such Republican virtues as frugality and integrity. During the Samnite War, enemy envoys approached the plebeian general Manius Curius Dentatus as he roasted turnips at his hearth. The Samnites offered heaps of gold if he would defect, but Dentatus stuck to his turnips and his country. This story illustrates the Roman genius for propaganda. Since the city's founding, clever politicians used *rapum* to show the common touch. At his accession, Romulus ate turnips to bond with the plebs, a custom revived by the Emperor Claudius, who composed a paean to the turnip. In fact, when Claudius died, the Senate deified him so that Romulus might share boiled turnips with someone on Olympus. Poor Remus had to settle for raw turnip greens in Hades.

Bitter but fortifying, turnip tops were consumed by slaves and scrub farmers. But, seasoned with fish sauce and garlic, these lowly greens were also popular on the Palatine. Even the most Hellenized patricians craved them, as if compelled to remind themselves that the capital of the world was once the poorest, weakest hamlet in Latium. *Rapum* curbed their appetite for power with wormwood. Supposedly, the bitterest turnip greens grew twenty kilometers southeast of the city on Mount Algidus, the rim of a dormant volcano and the site of Rome's Dunkirk, its humiliating defeat at the hands of the Aequi. Glory, history teaches, is neither inevitable nor permanent. The high noon of power always breeds shadows, just as abundant rain makes *rapum* go to weed.

When Rome fell, its vast turnip fields in Campania bolted and ran wild. Slowly, during the Middle Ages, cross-pollination and hybridization transformed *rapum* into rabe. Scientists, however, have never fully explained this metamorphosis, beginning with the eighteenth-century Swedish botanist Carl Linnaeus.

Linnaeus placed broccoli rabe within the order *Brassiceae,* family *Brassicaceae.* This group of veggies, which includes broccoli, Brussels sprouts, cabbage, cauliflower, kale, kohlrabi, mustard, radish, rutabaga, and turnip, is also called *Cruciferae,* cruciferous or cross-bearing plants, because of their cross-shaped leaves. Nicknamed crucifers, they pack an appropriately bitter taste and pave a Via Dolorosa on the tongue and esophagus. Technically, rabe belongs to the genus *Brassica,* species *Brassica rapa* or *campestris:* field or turnip mustard. But this classification dissatisfied Linnaeus, who proposed other designations: *Brassica rapa ruvo, Brassica rapa rapifera, Brassica ruvo, Brassica campestris ruvo.* What do you call a roaming plant whose florets resemble broccoli but whose taste is more pungent than mustard? To answer this riddle, Linnaeus should have consulted his older contemporary, the Neapolitan philosopher Giambattista Vico.

Before becoming the spaghetti capital of Europe, Naples was known for its passionate fondness for broccoli rabe or, as Neapolitans still prefer to call it, *friariello.* Professors claim the name is a corruption of the Spanish phrase *frios grelos* ("cold-hardy turnip tops"), a souvenir of four centuries of Hapsburg and Bourbon rule; ordinary people insist the name comes from the Neapolitan verb *frijere* ("to fry") because that is how the poor have always cooked rabe—fried in oil and eaten with bread.

But one fact is indisputable, states food historian John Dickey. For most of the sixteenth and seventeenth centuries, Neapolitans were nicknamed "leaf eaters," or, more pejoratively, "leaf shitters." Unashamed, Naples—always eager to promote tourism—brazenly cashed in on this notoriety through clever merchandising. Back in the 1690s, if you had thrown three threes while playing Cockaigne, Giuseppe Maria Mitelli's board game of city delicacies, you would have landed on the square labeled "Neapolitan broccoli," a mouth-watering bunch of rabe. No wonder a dialect poet exclaimed:

Oh leaf so tasty! Oh leaf so sweet!
You are our magnet, and our treat!

Like the blood of San Gennaro, rabe supposedly works miracles. Consumed in winter, it purifies the blood and lifts depression. As a summer homeopathy, it purges the bowels and regulates digestion. The leaves heal envy and ward off the evil eye, while the stems cure impotence and infertility. In the oldest version of the Rapunzel story, dating back to the early seventeenth century, a Neapolitan mother, embittered by years of barrenness, craves the rabe growing in a witch's garden. Her indulgent husband steals the greens, and the woman conceives and bears a daughter, Rapinella. This folk tale also testifies to rabe's hardiness. This plant will grow anywhere, even in a witch's backyard. But the real magic occurs in the kitchen.

ALTHOUGH ITALIANS prize broccoli rabe's bitterness, they must transform that bitterness to make it palatable. Like Horatian satire, rabe should sing, not scold, and so chefs tweak its indignation with the impudence of red pepper flakes or soften its rage with the sweetness of cippolini onions. Once mellowed, this savage misanthrope becomes the most civilized of dinner companions—but only with proper technique.

Cooking is the first step, whether by slow simmer or quick sauté. Since older bunches require more time to reduce their bite and soften their texture, chefs sometimes blanch broccoli rabe in boiling water for sixty to ninety seconds—just enough to mellow it without making it bland. But whether cooked to softness or barely wilted, rabe benefits greatly from three simple additions: salt, fat, and spice.

Salt takes the edge off any food's bitterness, but that's especially true with broccoli rabe, which possesses enough backbone to withstand the marshes of Ostia. Coarse sea salt works well, but cooks also use anchovies to season and add depth. When Attic wit fails, they turn unctuous. Fat, the great equalizer, curbs harsh tastes and fuses flavors on the palate. A dash of olive oil is enough to meld the assertive flavors of garlic, chile, and rabe, but why be subtle when you can add bacon or sausage? Whether mild and smoky or brash and greasy, pork best brings out rabe's unique flavor and texture.

New York's greatest Italian chefs—Mario Batali, Silvio Marchetto, Fabio Trabocchi, Tom Valenti—were raised on broccoli rabe, but, until recently, they seldom pushed the green on their uptown clientele. Maybe because this working-class staple is associated with too many painful childhood memories.

"My mother packed us some very exotic lunches compared to the other kids," recalls John De Lucie, chef and partner at the Wayverly Inn in the West Village. "There was broccoli rabe in my lunchbox and kids would make fun of me, saying that I was eating weeds."

To sample authentic rabe cuisine, therefore, cancel your reservation at Babbo in Greenwich Village and take the 6 train to Fratelli's Pizza Café in Hunts Point.

Located next to the Triangle Strip Club, Fratelli's caters to people who sling fish, trim beef, and wash greens all day. If Manhattan has more four-star restaurants and specialty groceries than any other city, if D'Agostinos stocks purple broccoli and Peter Luger serves three-inch-thick porterhouse steaks, it is because of the regulars at this South Bronx pizzeria, who work across the street at the world's largest wholesale market.

The Hunts Point Food Distribution Center occupies 329 square acres and contains nearly two million square feet of warehouse space. Each year, its three divisions—the New York City Terminal Market, the Hunts Point Cooperative Market, and the New Fulton Fish Market—supply two hundred thousand tons of meat, fish, and produce to restaurants and supermarkets throughout the country, generating $5 billion in revenue. The complex sits on a desolate peninsula jutting into the East River. Planes from LaGuardia take off directly across the water and roar low overhead. In addition, the one thousand delivery trucks daily rumbling in and out of the market cripple local traffic and cause asthma, but workers endure the noise and fumes.

"It's a blue-collar job engine," says co-operative co-president Matt D'Arrigo. "Thousands of guys come through—customers, drivers, and workers. You've got a real hardworking-man kind of mentality."

But if Hunts Point feeds Manhattan, Fratelli's Pizza Café feeds Hunts Point. Profiled by Sarah Di Gregorio in *The Village Voice*, Fratelli's is famous for its broccoli rabe specialties. A rabe hero glistens with a sheen of olive oil and comes on a soft roll, studded with golden-brown garlic cloves. A rabe-stuffed calzone steams and bursts. Penne and braised rabe somersault in a frying pan. A white pizza, topped with rabe florets, is placed on a wooden peel and shoved into a crowded oven.

If Fratelli's had opened on Staten Island, some marketer would have created a bumper sticker promoting "RABE POWER!" But the three Fratelli brothers, John, Joey, and Mario, who learned to cook from their immigrant parents, know such goombah gimmicks would fail in this war zone. Although the Hunts Point market employs twenty-five thousand people, few jobs are available for local residents, who, trapped in twenty crumbling blocks of row houses, projects, factories, refineries, and correctional facilities, resort to prostitution and drug dealing, neither of which requires a union card.

Sometimes the black strippers from next door will barge into Fratelli's, the sweat glistening on their cleavage, and demand broccoli rabe lasagna. John tells them to take it to the pole. "I don't know how they do it!" he marvels. "Eat a whole lasagna and dance the rest of the night!" He clutches his belly and laughs.

A sense of humor helps. Fratelli's hours are the same as the Hunts Point Market's: open from midnight on Sunday until midnight on Friday; closed on weekends. During the graveyard shift, the walls thump with music from the club. When business is slow, Mario flips through back issues of *Fortune* or gossips with gap-toothed whores. (If a hooker has good bridgework, Mario confides, she's probably undercover.) Even so, the long hours offer two advantages. First, the Fratellis can make long-simmered stocks and tomato sauces, because someone is always there to tend them. Second, being enmeshed with their suppliers guarantees the best ingredients and a steady stream of customers.

Matt D'Arrigo, who provides Fratelli's rabe, often lunches here. As he puts it: "It doesn't hurt, that's for sure, being right across the street."

He should know. His family got America to eat its greens.

WHEN SIXTEEN-YEAR-OLD Andrea D'Arrigo emigrated from Messina, Sicily, in 1904, passing through Ellis Island before settling in Boston, he brought only two things: the dream of making a new life in America and a small pouch of broccoli seeds. Unlike Jack in the Beanstalk, Andrea spoke no English, but hard work made the loneliness bearable until his younger brother Stefano arrived seven years later.

The D'Arrigo brothers learned English, earned engineering degrees, and joined the army in World War I. Andrea fought in France under General John J. Pershing, but even a personal reference from Black Jack himself would have been useless in the postwar job market. Forget engineering or, for that matter, construction. The brothers could not find work as organ grinders or ice-cream vendors. After a half-dozen aborted odd jobs, including being "hods" or cobblestone carriers, they joined a roadside farmers market. Back then, the produce industry consisted of the local summer season; for eight months of the year, fresh fruits and vegetables were unavailable. Andrea and Stefano would change that.

The two brothers loved produce. Perhaps it was in their blood. They partnered with their cousins in the Boston Fruit and Grape Company and learned the business. Stefano moved to California to direct the purchasing of grapes, while Andrea remained in Boston to sell. By 1923, they had broken with their cousins and started the D'Arrigo Brothers Company of Massachusetts, but their success resulted from California dreaming.

Drawn to the warmth of its strong Italian community, Stefano moved his wife and sons, Steve and Andy, to San Jose. Here and on scouting trips for grapes, Stefano found the produce of his childhood—broccoli, cardoon, fennel, and prickly pear—being grown by Sicilian immigrants. This discovery inspired the first trial planting of commercially grown broccoli from the still-vital seeds in Andrea's pouch. Later that year, the brothers pioneered the first transcontinental rail shipment of ice-packed broccoli from the West to the East Coast, but their greatest innovations were in marketing and advertising.

D'Arrigo Brothers took off in 1927, when the company began branding its California-grown broccoli with the Andy Boy label, featuring Stefano's eponymous, three-year-old son, whose soup-bowl haircut and winsome grin would become iconic. Each broccoli bunch came in a signature bright pink wrapper, containing recipes and cooking instructions. When the Empire State Building opened, Andy Boy hit the airwaves on New York radio stations, making history for being the first branded vegetable sponsor and for holding on-air cooking demonstrations.

As demand grew, Stefano sought a summer climate with a long growing season and introduced broccoli to the Salinas Valley. Eventually, the company's twenty-eight-acre operation would expand to twenty-five-thousand crop acres in two states, thanks to diversification. After World War II, it entered the lettuce market and, in the words of Jimmy Durante, "made a lot of *scarol*": escarole, but also money. By stocking ethnic specialties in early supermarkets, Andy D'Arrigo, who had succeeded father Stefano, conquered suburbia. His greatest accomplishment was introducing broccoli rabe in 1964. Visiting Sicily, he gathered seeds from wild mustard plants growing along the cliffs of Messina, crossed them with California turnip broccoli, patented the hybrid, and copyrighted the name. Everyone's favorite down-home green is also a corporate trademark.

During the sixties and seventies, Andy Boy's success ignited a minor culture war: leaf-eating Dagos versus meat-and-potato Anglos. Comedian Pat Cooper (born Pasquale Caputo) exploited this conflict in a raunchy night-club act.

After Pat's honeymoon, his Italian father visits and asks if the bride is pregnant. Pat demurs. He has been married for less than a month. What does Papa expect? A boy, that's what! And Pat can guarantee it if he eats broccoli. For seven years, Pat obeys until his tool becomes a bean pole. Pat finally begets a son, but the kid is born green.

"You know what we named him?" Pat says. "Andy Boy!"

Country-club Wasps cringed. It was bad enough these vulgarians had invaded the suburbs and served broccoli rabe at Fourth of July cookouts. A fifth column of Ivy League nutritionists, determined to turn Americans into rabbits, aided and abetted them. "It's broccoli, dear," wheedles the mother in a Carl Rose *New Yorker* cartoon. To which her recalcitrant tot retorts: "I say it's spinach, and I say the hell with it!"

When the white elite recaptured the country, produce became a hot-button issue. Upon becoming America's forty-first president, George Herbert Walker Bush banned broccoli from the White House and Air Force One. "I do not like broccoli," he announced at a press conference. "And I haven't liked it since I was a little kid and my mother made me eat it. And I'm President of the United States and I'm not going to eat any more."

Andy Boy protested by sending crates of broccoli to the Oval Office, but the First Lady unloaded the stash on various Washington food banks. Relations would not improve until her son Dubyuh posed with Broccoli Man, the mascot of the National Broccoli Growers Association, on the campaign trail.

"I like the tops," he told reporters, "but not the stalks."

After his election, Dubyuh sent Broccoli Man a thank-you card printed on Oval Office stationery. No other vegetable could boast about receiving a mash note from the White House, unless you count the corn and soy lobby, but Andy Boy had the last laugh. When Dubyuh visited Indonesia, a witch doctor threatened to turn him into a stalk of broccoli. The publicity department must have pinned the clipping on the bulletin board, if only to provide diversion from the company's chronic labor problems.

FOLLOWING CESAR CHAVEZ'S landmark 1970 strike, D'Arrigo Brothers signed a two-year contract with the United Farm Workers. The terms included a hiring hall, medical benefits, and wages that set a new standard for agricultural labor. But the company resented these concessions. Unlike other Salinas Valley growers, D'Arrigo Brothers was family owned and respected Latino culture. They hired workers the entire year and honored Catholic feast days. They were greasers, for Christ's sake, not gringos! When the UFW agreement expired, D'Arrigo refused to renegotiate.

Four years later, hoping to regain their losses, D'Arrigo workers—in one of the first representation elections held under the 1976 Agricultural Labor Relations Act—voted to unionize. For the next decade, workers harassed management. They wore UFW buttons in the fields. They marched through Salinas's streets to the D'Arrigo offices to back up negotiators. But fine print betrayed them. While the law obliged D'Arrigo to bargain with the union, it did not require the company to reach an agreement. Management was stalling until it could retaliate.

War was declared in 1998, the year of D'Arrigo Brothers' diamond jubilee. That summer, in late July, the company brought in machines. Broccoli rabe harvesters, who previously had worked at their own pace, now found themselves following a conveyor belt through the fields at a speed set by the machine. To pay the driver, the company cut its piece rate by ten cents.

According to D'Arrigo media spokesperson Nick Pascouli, the rabe harvesters could take the hit. Their wages, he claimed, ran between $8.81 and $15.23 an hour. "¡Mierda!" said Efrain Lara, the rabe cutter who headed the union. Workers made at most $60 on a good day and now would make less! Twenty-two years was an eternity to wait for a contract, but chiseling wages was the last straw. On August 5, Lara and his coworkers went on strike. At the time, D'Arrigo employed over nine hundred people in Salinas. Nearly six hundred walked out. Valley newspapers called the fray "The Rabe of Wrath."

Picketers congregated at dawn on the dirt roads leading deep into the fields south of Salinas, trying to keep the company from bringing in scabs to harvest its broccoli rabe. One morning, a week into the strike, picketers stopped the buses as they arrived. Other strikers opened the emergency doors. Cries of "¡Unanse! Come out with us!" filled the semidarkness as union supporters appealed to the scabs on board. Some climbed out with their dented lunch boxes. Others stayed in their seats, squirming, trying not to look out the window at the strikers below.

Monterey County sheriff's deputies arrived, forcing the picketers to let the buses through. Forming a line at the end of the road, the strikers called to the strikebreakers through bullhorns. Dogged union organizers followed the crews to the rabe field and remonstrated for an hour. As the strikers cheered, UFW organizer Jesus Corona, holding aloft a red-and-black flag, marched out of the field to the picket line, followed by a trail of workers who had decided not to break the strike.

"Every day we go visit D'Arrigo workers at home, to ask them to join us," said UFW vice-president Efren Barajas. "We find family after family living in garages, all over the valley. And they work all day for this company, every day. What does it say about the wages here, where you find people living in garages?"

As the strike entered its fourth week, tempers flared. Violence seemed inevitable, until a sudden tragedy reconciled the enemies. David D'Arrigo, Andy's forty-one-year-old son, was killed in a car accident on August 24. As a gesture to the family, the union suspended the strike and sent flowers to the wake. UFW representatives attended the funeral. The next day, strikers returned to the broccoli rabe fields under a back-to-work accord between the union committee and D'Arrigo Brothers. Grateful and chastened, the company agreed to provide health insurance and other benefits. Even so, rabe harvesters still work without a contact and must fight for every penny. On November 2, 2006, D'Arrigo Brothers settled a class-action law suit for $3.5 million, after a federal judge ordered the company to pay its workers for compulsory travel time on stifling field buses.

MEANWHILE, two thousand miles from Salinas Valley, broccoli rabe has become the Stalk of the Town. Naturally, Manhattan's trendiest Italian restaurants—Babbo, a block from Washington Square; Gustavio's, on East Fifty-ninth Street; Trattoria dell'Arte, across the street from Carnegie Hall—showcase this grace-note *contorno*. But other places, more interested in providing a setting for power lunches than preparing edible food, have co-opted the bitter green with more questionable results.

Fifty-Five Wall Street in the downtown Regent serves broccoli rabe on a bed of delicate lemon capellini. Spiked with shaved *bottarga* (cured fish roe) and spicy grilled radicchio and drowned in a garlicky Parmesan broth, it's too much of a good thing. Midtown's Le Cirque substitutes gnocchi for orecchiette in its rabe and sausage, which sits like a brick in the stomach, but diners can burn excess calories by flagging elusive waiters and shouting over Beacon Court chatter. Fred's at Madison Avenue, Barneys' in-house restaurant, charges ten bucks for braised rabe. Maybe that's because the chef wastes an entire cruet of olive oil on what should be a simple side dish.

How do working-class Italians in the outer boroughs react to this gentrification? With a peculiar mixture of irony and mockery that dates back to Horace. "*Nil admirari*," preached the poor kid from Apulia, who never forgot his roots even after becoming the Jay Leno of Augustan Rome. Don't buy the bullshit. If success comes, keep an outsider's perspective, a wiseguy's edge. Eat your rabe and razz the big shots.

The bitter laugh, Samuel Beckett reminds us, is the ethical laugh. But sarcasm can be a form of penance as well as protest. Despite good intentions, Italian Americans too often betray their ideals. We skimp on dues to pay for the Rat Pack's Las Vegas album. We idolize Vito Corleone, a fictitious gangster, but not Vito Marcantonio, the tribune of the American Labor Party, who for six terms represented what would become New York's Eighteenth Congressional District. Our college-educated grandchildren move to New Jersey, vote Republican, and oppose trade unions and immigration. Vicarious affluence makes us accept the sweet lies of upward mobility, until one of our own reminds us of the bitter truth.

Speaking on behalf of the great Empire State and the whole family of New York, then governor Mario Cuomo addressed the 1984 Democratic Convention. How ironic, he noted, to hold this event in San Francisco, the city named after the patron of the poor, when the past four years had marked a return to the Gilded Age and Social Darwinism. According to the new dispensation, government should take care of the strong and hope that economic ambition and charity will do the rest. Make the rich richer, and whatever falls from the table will be enough for the working poor trying to gain a toe-hold in the middle class. Cuomo ridiculed this "wagon train" mentality, alluding to Ronald Reagan. Before entering politics, Reagan had hosted the TV series *Death Valley Days*. Now the former pitchman for Borateen, the 20-Mule-Team detergent, sold supply-side economics.

From the portico of the White House and the veranda of his ranch, President Reagan saw only opportunity and prosperity. But in other parts of the Promised Land, Cuomo said, homeowners couldn't pay their mortgages, students couldn't afford college, the elderly trembled in their basements, ghetto kids succumbed to drugs, the homeless slept in the gutter, and rabe harvesters worked without a contact. The struggle for dignity, not the cult of celebrity, is the real story of America. Cuomo didn't read this story in a book or learn it in a classroom. He memorized it in a grocery in South Jamaica, Queens, helping his immigrant father open crates of greens:

"I watched a small man with thick calluses on both his hands work fifteen and sixteen hours a day. I saw him once literally bleed from the bottoms of his feet, a man who came here uneducated, alone, unable to speak the language, who taught me all I needed to know about faith and hard work by the simple eloquence of his example. I learned about our kind of democracy from my father. And I learned about our obligation to each other from him and from my mother. They asked only for a chance to work and to make the world better for their children, and they asked to be protected in those moments when they would not be able to protect themselves."

Once upon a time, government defended working people. Perhaps if Cuomo had not played Hamlet on the Hudson, it would have returned to this mission. Instead, we got nearly three decades of corporate welfare and federal bailouts, and America became a frat house. If you want to belong, taunted the Masters of the Universe, you must rush, pledge, and bend over for the paddle. Endure enough humiliation, affect enough scorn, and you too can earn the privilege of hazing newcomers. If that is what assimilation means, Italian Americans should reject it. At stake are our very souls.

Whenever we clamor to build a high-tech wall along the Mexican border or to enforce stricter racial profiling at airports, let us recall our own history of discrimination. *"You shall not oppress the alien,"* God commands the Israelites in the Book of Exodus, *"for you yourselves know how it feels to be an alien, because you were aliens in Egypt."* To be truly free, one must remember slavery; one must eat bitter greens in the land of milk and honey. Jews use endive at Passover, Italians broccoli rabe at Sunday dinner. No matter how hard we try to uproot it, it grows in our heart and stays on our plate.

DOLCE

*Sicilian Chocolate
Cake*

Dark Chocolate

SICILIAN
CHOCOLATE CAKE

IF YOU CAN'T STAND THE HEAT, stay out of the Sicilian kitchen! But this refreshing dessert requires no baking, a relief during Sicily's dog days, when temperatures reach 110 degrees in the shade.

The original recipe calls for Crema di Ricotta, which takes two whole days to prepare. Whipped cream laced with vanilla, however, makes an acceptable substitute.

INGREDIENTS
- 4 large eggs, brought to room temperature
- 1 cup sugar
- ¾ cup unsweetened cocoa powder
- 2 cups crumbled butter biscuits or cookies
- 1 ¼ cups melted butter, plus an extra stick for coating the pan
- 2 cups whipped cream, blended with 1 teaspoon vanilla extract
- ½ teaspoon cinnamon

DIRECTIONS
1. Beat the eggs and sugar in a large bowl. Stir in the cocoa and blend well.
2. Add the biscuit crumbs and mix, then add the melted butter.
3. Coat 9 x 4 inch loaf pan with extra butter. Fit pieces of parchment paper to bottom and sides and press firmly in place. Turn mixture into pan and lightly press down.
4. Cover the pan and refrigerate overnight.
5. When ready to serve, invert the cake onto a work surface and carefully remove paper. As an extra touch,

heat a long, straight-edged knife and pass it over the
tip and sides of the cake to bring a shine.

6. Slice cake and top with vanilla-flavored cream. Sprinkle with cinnamon.

This dessert is so sinfully delicious it requires a church indulgence
for Catholics. I recommend petitioning the Bishop of Ragusa.
Modica, Sicily's chocolate capital, falls under his jurisdiction.

DARK CHOCOLATE

"SWEETS TO THE SWEET," cooed Dr. Delvecchio. I giggled when he rattled what appeared to be a jar of jelly beans, until I realized—with a gasp—that the treats were Grandpa's severed toes. The rest of the clan remained silent. After enduring months of pranks and lies, Doc had earned the right to play rough. He leaned over the mahogany desk—his neck cords tautening, his flattop bristling, his turkey wattle quivering—and confronted Grandpa. "Didn't I order you to stop eating candy? Didn't I warn you this would happen? Now suffer!" he spat.

Like a tortoise, Grandpa retracted his head, licked his lips, and sulked. Frustrated, Doc glanced at the phrenological head on his desk then turned to my aunts and mother. Even when calm, he spoke in a reedy, hectoring voice, and Doc was far from calm. If Harry Truman had been Sicilian, the three sisters once joked, he would have sounded like Anthony J. Delvecchio. Accusingly, Doc leveled his pipe at the oldest, Aunt Rose. Although he had quit smoking before I was born, he still sucked the residual tobacco under stress. The pipe stem, I noticed, was covered with tooth marks. Half of them caused by Grandpa.

"You have nothing to say?" Doc asked.

Rose shrugged. Having rejected a gangster's son, despite repeated death threats, this flinty spinster was not about to be intimidated by a mere MD. Just because Doc ran the richest practice on Seventy-sixth Street, didn't make him God. "What can we do? He's a grown man."

"A grown infant!" Doc snapped.

"We should keep him in a crib?"

Grandpa snickered. Humped and shriveled, he was no bigger than a ten-year-old. Sharing the same seat, he and I must have seemed like playmates rather than grandfather and grandson. Doc caught the old man's catty smile and regained his composure.

"No," he said, "but you should restrain him."

"How?" Rose demanded. "All of us work, even Mamma! Somebody's got to in this cockamamie family!"

Grandma's martyred expression confirmed this report. A widow-in-training, she wore a black church dress and worried a rosary. Nodding, Doc acknowledged Grandma's shame and suffering but pursued his point: "Then hire someone to supervise him."

Rose snorted. "With every penny going for insulin? Not likely, mister!"

Mamma interrupted. The last to leave Sicily, she was the least Americanized, the most respectful. "The neighbors look in, but it's no good, *dottore*. He sneaks to the corner newsstand and buys chocolate."

"But don't the exercise help?" asked pug-faced Aunt Giovanna.

Dr. Delvecchio sighed as if he were expelling the last breath of patience on earth. Circulation, he explained, for the hundredth time, wasn't the problem. Nerve damage had left Grandpa so impervious to pain that he no longer could gauge his condition. The foot had turned gangrenous. Already the remaining toes looked and smelled like rotted olives. If the infection were not contained, the entire foot would need to be amputated, maybe even the leg below the knee, so it was imperative to lower Grandpa's blood sugar.

As the adults consulted, I saw Grandpa remove a half-melted Ghirardelli bar from inside his flannel shirt. He put a finger to his lips, unwrapped the bar, broke off a sliver, and slipped the shard into his mouth. Even before losing his teeth, he never chewed chocolate but let it melt on his tongue like the Host. Bliss transformed his ravaged face and erased all traces of suffering and disappointment. But his smacking lips got everyone's attention. Aunt Rose stifled a chuckle. Mamma and Aunt Giovanna shook their heads. Grandma recited the Seven Sorrowful Mysteries. But Dr. Delvecchio was a monument to outrage. In the glow of the Mission lamp, his gold spectacles gleamed; his mouth gaped like a carp's on crushed ice.

Grandpa opened his eyes and smirked. Chocolate trickled down his chin. Quaking, Doc noticed the picture of his only child Angelina, a moon-faced Sister of the Sacred Heart, and laid the photo facedown on his desk before he exploded. Roaring obscenities, he hammered the phrenological head with his pipe. When the pipe shattered and the head chipped, he hurled against the wall a calfskin appointment book, a bronze letter opener, and a coral paperweight, a souvenir from his silver anniversary trip to Capri.

Throughout this rampage, Grandpa laughed while the rest of us ducked for cover. Finally, Doc spluttered and collapsed in a leather swivel chair. For a moment, he mutely appealed to the artifacts gracing his office—the complete edition of Croce, the Piranesi prints, the Toscanini LPs—then declared: "This is pointless. No doctor can help a patient determined to die." Hanging his head, he pointed to the door. The appointment was over. But before we left, Grandpa patted Doc's hand and said, "Don't take it so hard. It's fate."

Four months later, Grandpa was dead. A contrarian to the end, he deliberately cut off his nose to spite his face; or, rather, cut off his toes to spite his foot. For seventy-three years, he had defied priests and *carabinieri*, bankers and bosses, traffic cops and trolley conductors. Only God was left, and in their cosmic standoff, Grandpa's last name proved all too apt. Bilo, a corruption of the Italian word for "bile," also means "gall" or "spleen." When a man is *bilioso*, he is possessed by a spiteful pride that doubles down when it should fold. Grandpa would burn down his house to fry his eggs. He always picked the wrong fight, bet on the wrong horse, backed the wrong cause. Perverse ingenuity had transformed his life into a series of perfectly executed fiascos. The guy could lose at solitaire.

And yet, we seldom blamed him. If Grandpa was addicted to failure as much as candy, both addictions were more cultural than personal. Sugar is to Sicily what whisky is to Ireland: an escape from bleak reality into a world of pure imagination. For millennia, kings and commoners, revolutionaries and reactionaries, mobsters and cobblers have sweetened the bitterness of futility with Attic honey and Roman jam, Turkish marzipan and Mexican cocoa. Comfits comfort us, and we spin dreams like cotton candy until we awake and die. Disillusioned with philosophy, Empedocles leapt into Mount Etna. Disappointed by America, Grandpa plunged into a vat of dark chocolate.

DOMENICO BILO WAS BORN on May 3, 1891, Machiavelli's birthday, so perhaps he was destined to outfox himself. He came from Villabate, then an agricultural center of ten thousand inhabitants. For two hundred years, Menico's family had been tenant farmers here, ever since Antonio Agnello, an aristocratic abbé and an amateur botanist, founded a commune to develop the hardy strands of olive and citrus that became the area's chief crops. Most of the town, in fact, had been parceled from the abbé's huge estate, hence the name, Villabate. The Agnello family chapel, with its gold tympanum, still stands, but a century ago, sightseers from nearby Palermo also toured an arboretum and ornate greenhouses. As they promenaded by the bandstand, to party music from *La Traviata*, these well-tailored visitors tantalized young Menico. Forced to share a threadbare dress shirt with three older brothers, the boy attended church only once a month. Nevertheless, he still dreamed of an earthly paradise. Everybody did. It was the Age of Innocence.

A twenty-year boom at the turn of the last century gave Sicily a fleeting taste of prosperity. Like most gilded eras, this one was based on denial. Turning its back on the Fasci Siciliani, a failed populist uprising of sulfur miners and field hands, and ignoring widespread migrations and deportations to America, society basked in a delayed but sunny Belle Époque. New money—represented by the Tascas and Florios, Sicily's shipping and Marsala tycoons—had conquered and married into the old aristocracy. Determined to prove their backward island belonged to a progressive, united Italy, these merchant princes modernized the capital.

Menico marveled as Palermo expanded outside the old city walls along the Via della Libertà. This new boulevard boasted numerous villas in Stile Liberty. Named after the Chesham fabric manufacturer and retailer Arthur Lasenby Liberty, Stile Liberty crossed John Wanamaker with William Morris. Overnight Palermo's northwest side became an American emporium designed by the English Arts and Crafts Movement. The presiding genius of this new architectural style, Ernesto Basile, built the Teatro Massimo, the city's new opera house, and Villa Igeia: once a retreat for the Florio family, now a deluxe hotel. He also reconstructed popular taste.

On weekend trolley rides, Menico noted the city's changing fashions. Spanish Baroque was out, Art Nouveau was in. Proper families required a French chef and an English governess. Fashionable young men sported London tailoring and smoked Virginia cigarettes. Even traditional desserts received a makeover. Up to this point, all classes shamelessly enjoyed the pastries from Palermo's ancient convents. The products of a fortified but hysterical virginity, these confections bore such suggestive names as Virgin's Breasts, Chancellor's Buttocks, Saint Lucy's Eyes, and Bones of the Dead. Made for major religious festivals, convent pastries were sponsored by the aristocracy and distributed to the peasants in the country. But the bourgeoisie, who considered such sweets the relics of a priest-ridden past, preferred a new alternative.

Exploiting and embodying Palermo's *dolce vita*, confectioners had begun selling the first commercial pastries. The Gulì brothers transformed their basement candy factory into an elegant tearoom and pastry shop in Piazza Marina, glittering with chandeliers, candy vases of imported Bohemian crystal, and display cases of multi-tiered *cassate*. In the spirit of free trade, Swiss *patissiers* were encouraged to establish competing businesses. Selling never-before-seen babàs, brioches, and chocolates, the Caflisch family also copied traditional convent pastries. Despite protests from the old guard, many customers preferred the machine-made substitutes to the handmade originals because they were perfectly formed and cheaply plentiful. But the Willa Wonka of Sicily was Francesco Bonajuto, the man who had modernized the island's ancient art of chocolate making and inadvertently corrupted my grandfather.

Bonajuto was from Modica, Sicily's fabled chocolate capital. Located in the southeastern province of Ragusa, Modica straddled a gorge in the Iblean Mountains. Shaped by four hills, it was divided into two parts—Modica Alta, whose amber-colored buildings scaled the cliffs, and Modica Bassa, at the bottom of the valley—and joined by a maze of streets and steps. The town was breathtaking, but its precarious beauty was menaced by distant Mount Etna. On January 11, 1693, an earthquake devastated the entire region, killing twenty-four hundred *modicani*. Rising from the ashes, the town never forgot that sudden disaster. How could it, when its splendid Baroque buildings, its walks and streets, were built from or cobbled with the rubble?

But until 1902, flood had menaced as often as fire. Once Modica was the Venice of Sicily; its many bridges had spanned the Ianni Mauro and Pozzo dei Pruni, which joined the Monticano River and flowed into the Noto Valley. But after a deluge, engineers diverted and filled the two streams to create Corso Umberto, the town's main avenue and historic center.

Now the only thing flowing through Modica was an Arno of chocolate.

DARK AND ACRID, Modican chocolate is unadulterated by the milk of human kindness; its atavistic flavor replicates that of *xocoàtl,* the Mexican cocoa first brought to Europe in 1528. Perhaps the most prized booty of the Spanish conquest, more refined in its cruelty than cocaine, *xocoàtl* was a product of war and extortion. The Maya, who flourished eight centuries before Cortez, venerated this black gold, as evident from the ornate chocolate vessels, made of clay, found in their tombs. According to myth, Quetzalcoatl the Plumed Serpent bestowed cacao to the Maya after the divine grandmother goddess Xmucane created humans from maize. The grateful Maya held a festival each April for the cacao god, Ek Chuah, whose headdressed priests offered feathers and incense before sacrificing a dog with cacao-colored markings. *Xocolatl* (literally, "bitter water") became a sacramental wine. Throughout the Yucatan and other coastal areas, cocoa consecrated Mayan weddings. To seal their union, a bride and groom would drink chocolate from a common goblet.

But for the Aztecs, who dominated central Mexico, cocoa symbolized the power and glory of their vast empire. The god kings demanded a yearly tribute of 980 loads of cacao, painstakingly counted out into twenty-four thousand beans per load. The proceeds provided the chocolate that capped Montezuma's lavish banquets, as well as the household staples sold in Tenochtitlan's crowded markets. Cacao was also used as currency: four beans could buy a wild turkey, one hundred a slave. Not surprisingly, counterfeiting was rampant. Swindlers would stuff cacao shells with clay or packed earth, despite the penalty of dismemberment.

Officials rarely enforced the law, however, because such chicanery targeted the poor, who would drink mud if the priests told them it was *xocoàtl*. Naturally, merchants reserved the finest cocoa for the rich, who flavored their drinks with sesame, anise, vanilla, allspice, ground corn, honey, and chiles.

Royal chocolate, however, contained various dried and powdered aromatic flowers with special properties. Before the emperor visited his harem, palace chefs laced his cocoa with an extract of magnolia mexicana, to enhance potency. Using a *molinillo,* a wooden stick with a fluted head, they whipped the mixture into a creamy froth and served it to Montezuma, who, toasting the fertility goddess Xochiquetzalli, quaffed fifty golden cups of this elixir at one sitting. Each sip, he told his Spanish guests, brought wisdom and vitality. But not all libations, the conquistadors discovered, were innocent. The Aztecs served cocoa to sacrificial victims before eviscerating them. This custom came from the Maya, whose cooks sometimes added achiote, a dark red seasoning paste, to their chocolate to produce a deep red color. Most likely, this dark red seasoning substituted for human blood.

These rituals revolted the Spanish, but they quickly succumbed to chocolate because of its caffeine. Writing to Charles V in 1519, Cortez reported, "A cup of this miraculous beverage gives every soldier the strength to march for an entire day." This effect should not surprise us. Chocolate was the first stimulant these Europeans had encountered, decades before coffee or tea. A sixteenth-century Italian traveler, who smuggled cocoa back to Florence, claimed the New World Spanish were "addicted" to chocolate. Actually, they were hooked on greed. When a triumphant Cortez returned to Madrid, chamberlains stockpiled cocoa beans in an underground vault, along with gold, jewels, and painted skulls. Entrusted with the Aztec recipe, monasteries processed the beans and kept chocolate a lucrative state secret for nearly a century.

To maximize profits, Spain planted cocoa trees in Sicily, an Aragonese fiefdom for two hundred years. That was how Modica became the empire's most important chocolate center after Alicante. Philip II granted the town a corporate charter for three reasons: its unquestioning loyalty to the crown; its North African climate, so similar to that of the Mesoamerican peninsula; and its plentiful supply of lava stone, essential for preparing chocolate the ancient Aztec way. The resulting prosperity transformed Modica. Spanish chroniclers called the city "an island within the island, a kingdom within the kingdom," and the provincial nobility, the Chiaramonte, the Cabrera, and the Henriquez, became notorious for their extravagance. Lords dined on such exotic dishes as 'mpanatigghi, a bizarre but delicate blend of raw mincemeat and cocoa, and u lebbru 'nciucculattatu, wild rabbit cooked in chocolate. Ladies drank hot cocoa in church, even during Lent, claiming it prevented fainting during high mass.

A Dominican priest denounced the practice. Drinking chocolate in church violated the fast laws, he thundered from the pulpit. Noblewomen and their entourage boycotted his church, and an assassin dispatched the impertinent cleric with a mug of poisoned chocolate. The scandal prompted the Archbishop of Syracuse to consult Pope Alexander VII, who in 1662 declared: "Liquidum non frangit jejunum." Liquids (including chocolate) do not break a fast.

By the eighteenth century, the Spanish empire had vanished, but the ciucculattari still ruled. Soliciting door-to-door in Modica's most affluent neighborhoods, these vendors pushed colorful carts containing pre-roasted cocoa beans; sugar, vanilla, cinnamon, and spices; a stone bowl and pestle; and a charcoal brazier. They ground, mixed, and seasoned the beans to order and then heated the powder until the cocoa butter melted, but before the sugar fully dissolved. Poured into a tin mold, the goop hardened into a crystal-studded bar. Thus street peddlers preserved Modica's aristocratic chocolate, albeit in a diminished and domesticated form.

THE BONAJUTO FAMILY had been ciucculattari for four generations, until Federico Bonajuto in 1827 upgraded his pushcart into a small pastry shop. His son Francesco, nicknamed Ciccio, transformed the store into a regional enterprise. Mass-production methods introduced at the dawn of the nineteenth century had transformed chocolate manufacture. The steam engine made ground cocoa beans to produce large amounts of chocolate cheaply and quickly. Greater quantities reduced steep prices, and for the first time the masses could afford chocolate.

Ciccio's small factory, built in 1880, applied the Industrial Revolution to *cioccolato modicano* but without compromising quality. Although innovation had its place, some traditions were sacrosanct. For example, Bonajuto bucked the new trend set by Daniel Peter and omitted milk. Let the Swiss suck their mother's tits! Sicilians craved the taste of catastrophe. Likewise, he avoided conching, refining, and mellowing his chocolate in a shell-shaped container of beads. He wanted his product to be gritty and bold. A perfectionist, Bonajuto controlled every stage of production, from growing his own cacao trees to designing and distributing his own advertising, and his face became as familiar in Italian stores as King Umberto's. In 1911, he won the Grand Gold Medal at Rome's International Exhibition. My grandfather cheered, and Palermo and Catania celebrated with fireworks.

But not everyone rejoiced at Bonajuto's success. Old Red Shirts and young Communists considered Sicily's chocolate craze decadent, a frivolity typifying the age's betrayal of heroic political action. Even the most ambitious and energetic Tancredi, they mumbled, become a lotus eater after eating a Bonajuto bar. Not all the absinthe served at the Palermo Palmes, not all the opium distilled from the poppies in Enna, softened the brain like Bonajuto chocolate. They were right. I have tasted Modican chocolate only once, and the experience nearly killed me.

Used to the bland Hershey bars of suburban New Jersey, I expected something smooth and mild. Instead, when I bit into the crunchy outer shell, I found myself chewing a granola of honeyed beetles. Numerous sugar crystals numbed my palate, while a raw powder—thick and pasty as volcanic ash—paralyzed my tongue. Traumatized, my taste buds recoiled and stumbled into a mine field of red pepper flakes, cloves, nutmeg, and allspice. Just as the agony became unbearable, molten velvet soothed my tongue, and a warm bliss settled on me like the descent of the Holy Ghost. For all I knew, I had experienced Nirvana. The shock obliterated my will and consciousness, and I gladly drowned in an ocean of chocolate. Shipwreck was sweet in such a sea.

But when the rush subsided, I felt miserable. From a god, I reverted to a worm. That is the danger of Sicilian chocolate. "Tasting Modican chocolate," explains the novelist Leonardo Sciascia "is like reaching a Platonic archetype, the absolute. Chocolate produced elsewhere, even the most celebrated, is an adulteration, a corruption of the original." And the physical world itself becomes a dingy shadow of the ideal. At that moment, I understood my grandfather. His self-destructive craving was a hunger for transcendence, but he had never recognized it, much less fed it. Instead, he associated chocolate with success, and success with immortality. This mistake proved fatal. Before it killed him, chocolate made Grandpa Dominic marry above his station, abandon Sicily, ruin a promising career, and sell himself to a thug.

ON FEBRUARY 21, 1912, during Mardi Gras in Palermo, twenty-one-year-old Domenico Bilo met Agata Bilo, the daughter of Villabate's most powerful burgher and landlord. With her slate-colored eyes, thick eyebrows, and severe bun secured with an ivory comb, fifteen-year-old Agata seemed a postulant without an order. Because she would not smile, Menico turned a cartwheel in the square and captivated the austere beauty. The lad's patchwork clothes and glib manner reminded her of a Harlequin in a street play, but when Agata realized the rags were no costume, she fled. Overtaking the girl in the crushing, giddying crowd, Menico offered her a half-eaten Bonajuto bar.

"One bite," she later confessed, "sealed my fate."

Nonna blamed God. I blame chemicals. As every scientist and *Redbook* editor knows, dark chocolate contains a bitter alkaline called theobromine. Literally meaning "food of the gods," theobromine stimulates the nervous system and induces euphoria. Subtler but longer lasting than those of its cousin caffeine, theobromine's properties are spiked by sugar, which releases serotonin into the brain. Hence chocolate's power as an aphrodisiac. For a young girl with no mother and a strict father, enjoying a rare taste of license before another oppressive Lent, the experience must have shattered her. Love rocked Agata like the Messina earthquake.

Fearing her father Don Nino, the lovers limited their first encounters to the steps of Santa Madre, Villabate's Baroque church dedicated to Agata's namesake. After mass, Menico would smuggle chocolates into the girl's pocket. Later they rendezvoused at the Spanish lookout towers on the nearby Castellammare Gulf or took secret walks in Palermo's municipal parks. But Don Nino discovered the affair one evening when a hayseed mandolinist serenaded his daughter beneath her balcony. The irate patriarch emptied a bedpan on the lover's head and ordered his daughter to break off the relationship.

Emboldened by love, or perhaps maddened by chocolate, Agata convinced Menico to elope. Three months later, Don Nino's spies tracked the newlyweds to a flour mill in Trapani. Making the best of a bad situation, Don Nino searched for a suitable position for his son-in-law. Learning Menico used to sell sumac to the village tanner, Don Nino apprenticed him to Varesi, an upscale shoe store on Palermo's Via della Libertà.

"Since you seem hell-bent for leather," the old man said, "maybe you'll make a good cobbler."

Menico resented the favor. At home, he browbeat Agata, mocked his in-laws, and splurged on Bonajuto. But at work, he gradually became a professional. Craftsmanship and camaraderie tempered his rebelliousness, and he savored the elegant surroundings: the plate-glass window, the Tiffany lamps, the Bugatti screen, the parquet floor. Under the *padrone*'s sunny tutelage, Menico blossomed. His hands were nimble and sure, whether cutting leather or distributing chocolate bars to bashful society girls, who blushed whenever he peeled their foil.

He had secured a full-time job as a patternmaker at Spattafori, a more prestigious boutique, when Italy entered the Great War. The Army drafted and shipped Menico to the Austrian front, where shrapnel riddled his forehead. The absurdity and futility of trench warfare reawakened his insubordination, so when the government offered the disgruntled veteran a low-level factory job or free passage to America, he chose America. Taking a steamer to Naples, he worked the docks until he had earned enough money to pay for his passage on the *Guglielmo Pierce*.

Dominic Bilo arrived in New York on Christmas Day, 1920. The passenger manifest lists his height as five feet, his complexion as dark. The clerk noted his brown hair, brown eyes, and scarred forehead. With only twenty-five dollars cash in his pocket, he sought his brainy brother-in-law, Giovanni Coffaro, who had come to America ten years earlier and now resided on 383 Marion Street in the Bushwick section of Brooklyn, a block from

Chauncey Street. Already a tool-and-die operator at the Ronzoni factory on Thirty-fifth Street and Northern Boulevard in Long Island City, Giovanni held an engineering degree from the University of Palermo and would patent several pasta-making machines. The budding inventor always brought home free boxes of spaghetti, but his generosity and good luck choked Dominic, who could find no dignified work and had settled for the dirtiest and most mind-numbing construction jobs. Exhaustion stupefied him, until he discovered the Irish foreman was underpaying him. When Dom asked why, the boss replied, "Because you're a pig."

Resentment spurred initiative. Since none of the German shoe merchants on Knickerbocker Avenue would hire him, Dominic took his hammer, awl, and last across the Williamsburg Bridge. Moving to 383 East Broadway on the Lower East Side, he found part-time work at various Jewish repair shops on Delancey, Orchard, and Kenarsey. Within two years, he felt confident enough to acquire a passport, but he never became a citizen. His American sojourn seemed too tenuous. But a lucky break ended this hand-to-mouth existence. Through the grapevine, his talents became known to Izzy Miller, the Shoemaker of Show Biz. After a breezy interview, Dom found himself a master craftsman at I. Miller Shoes on Broadway. This was the highpoint of my grandfather's life. At last, he could satisfy his appetite for fame and glory, and Signor Miller would treat him like a son. He and Dom were two of a kind.

A COBBLER FROM POLAND, Israel Miller came to New York in 1892 and began making shoes for theatrical productions. His designs became so popular that many vaudevillians turned to him to produce their personal footwear. In 1911 he opened a small store in a brownstone at 1552 Broadway at Forty-sixth Street, which soon expanded into the adjacent property at 1554 Broadway. Showrooms were constructed on the upper floors of both buildings.

Drawing on his years at Varesi and Spattafori, Dominic suggested ways to improve the décor. He also recommended giving free chocolate to the ladies. Impressed, Izzy began cultivating the young Sicilian. He needed help running his empire. By the time he bought the property in 1926, I. Miller Shoes not only had become America's most popular designer and manufacturer of women's shoes but a leading importer with a national chain of over two hundred retail stores, a position the company retained for the next forty years.

To celebrate, Izzy hired architect Louis H. Freeland, who unified the buildings' facades, using marble with granite trim and bronze fittings around the showcase windows. Niches were added along the wall to honor New York's four favorite divas. With Dom's help, Izzy released a public ballot to pick representative stars from drama, musical comedy, opera, and film. Miller then commissioned Alexander Sterling Calder to make Art Deco sculptures of the winners: Ethel Barrymore as Ophelia, Marilyn Miller as Sunny, Rosa Ponselle as Norma, and Mary Pickford as Little Lord Fauntleroy. The wall along West Forty-sixth Street, beneath the cornice, still bears the inscription "THE SHOW FOLKS SHOE SHOP DEDICATED TO BEAUTY IN FOOTWEAR."

It was a sweet deal, but Dom soured it. A bit of a nooge, Izzy sometimes rubbed him the wrong way. Shine those patent-leather pumps again, will you, kid? No, no, no! The snakeskin, not the alligator skin! One day, nursing a headache from eating too many chocolates, Dom lost his temper and quit. Izzy begged him to reconsider. The Stock Market had crashed. Now was the worst time to leave. Dom didn't care. Using his savings, he opened his own store and shoe repair shop on Canal Street. Despite the Depression, business was brisk, thanks to the Mafiosi who wanted to look sharp. The hoods called Dom the St. Crispin of Little Italy. Unfortunately, his success attracted the attention of Boss Joe Masseria, who wanted a piece of the action.

At first, because Dom had made him a beautiful pair of spats, Joe was diplomatic. He visited the store without bodyguards, accepted a chocolate bar, and briefed Dom on the international situation. Dom was caught in the crossfire of the so-called Castellammare War, the blood feud between Masseria and his Brooklyn rival Salvatore Maranzano, who had been sent by Don Vito Cascioferro of Palermo to undermine the New York boss. Maranzano had established rival enterprises, which were siphoning Masseria's profits. Dom chewed his chocolate. What did this have to do with him? Well, technically, Joe explained, Dom was a Brooklynite, so his setting up shop on Canal Street might be considered an affront. Only technically, mind you. But if Dom pledged his undying loyalty, limited his trade to the Masseria Family and its clients, and offered the proper tribute, all would be forgiven.

Joe's flattery and promises of protection fell on deaf ears. Dom wasn't interested in paying a monthly fee. That night, someone broke into his shop and cut the tongues off his shoes. When that didn't work, goons sliced out pieces from Dom's tongue and trashed his business. With blood streaming from his mouth, he fled Lower Manhattan and never again crossed the Brooklyn Bridge again. The maimed fugitive settled on eighteenth Avenue in Bensonhurst, near the Alba Pastry Shop. But Brooklyn was no haven. Enforcers had put the word on the street. No one was to hire Dominic Bilo. Broke, he cabled Nonna Agata to send their three oldest daughters, Francesca, Rosa, and Giovanna. He didn't want consolation so much as cheap labor.

While the girls supported Dom, the Castellammare War ended. Gunmen had assassinated Joe Masseria at the Nuova Villa Tammaro restaurant in Coney Island, making Salvatore Maranzano *capo di tutti i capi,* boss of all the bosses. But his reign proved short. At a catered meeting in the Bronx, the classically educated Maranzano proposed reorganizing the American mob based on Caesar's legions. Sleek and vulpine, he quoted Machiavelli and sprinkled his speech with Latin. Raising his arms, Don Maranzano intoned, "*Sursum corda!*" Lift up your hearts! And like sullen boys at their First Communion, five hundred gangsters filed in line to kiss his ring and lick a chocolate *cannolo*. Lucky Luciano bristled. Did this Moustache Pete want him to suck his cock? Five months later, he hurled Maranzano from his ninth-floor office in the Helmsley Building and made Joseph Profaci, Maranzano's lieutenant, don of Brooklyn.

Born in Villabate, Profaci was distantly related to the Bilos. When my aunts learned their *compare* had come to power, they nagged their father to ask for a favor. Proud and wary, Dom didn't want to be indebted to anyone, least of all a Mafioso, but when he became sick of polenta and calf liver, he made overtures. He offered to repair the don's custom-made shoes for nothing. The results pleased Profaci. They were better than new. Why wasn't Dom employed? A long story, Dom said. The don printed Dom some business cards for his next round of interviews: "*Joe Profaci wants to know when I can go to work.*" But Dom couldn't keep a job. Never again, he vowed, would he bust his ass for anyone, not even his family, whom he treated as indentured servants. A traditionalist, he honored the old proverb: "The cobbler's children go barefoot."

AT THIS POINT, the entire clan was reunited, my mother and grandmother having arrived in 1946. The extra income made it possible to move from a basement apartment on Seventy-ninth Street to a charming turn-of-the-century duplex at 1459 Eightieth Street, a block and a half from New Utrecht High. The school's Dickensian brick façade would be featured in the opening credits of the seventies sit-com *Welcome Back, Kotter,* but for now these words from William Pitt were carved over its entrance: "WHERE LAW ENDS, TYRANNY BEGINS." Ironic, considering the Profacis controlled Dyker Heights. But the school produced another breed of wiseguys. Jackie Gleason, Phil Silvers, and the Three Stooges all graduated from New Utrecht High: chiselers, dreamers, and clowns, just like my grandfather.

Although he kept a small shop under the New Utrecht el, Grandpa mostly loafed. Whenever Mamma brought him an artichoke *frittata* for lunch, the door was always closed. She would buzz and buzz until he opened up, his face swollen from napping on a back-room cot. Eventually, he abandoned the shop and freelanced out of the apartment, quite happy to be supported by four women. Normally, such conduct would have made him a pariah. And indeed, the landlord, Signor Benza, treated him with contempt. Despite being Sid Caesar's high-school pal, Benza was not amused by his upstairs tenant, whose childish antics had driven away Francesca. Benza called Grandpa a *menefreghista,* a man who didn't give a fuck.

But the neighborhood adored him. Grandpa was a character. His damaged tongue slurred his speech, so he compensated by mangling old vaudeville routines and playing his mandolin, an antique Calace, a gift from Don Profaci. Oddly, his impediment never affected his singing. Publicly, he was a lovable ne'er-do-well, a prankster who once invited a gossipy widow for tea and had her sit on a stool coated with cement glue, but privately he was a morose and embittered man. His one consolation was Ghirardelli chocolate.

Domenico Ghirardelli was the American Bonajuto. Grandpa hero-worshipped him, not the least because they shared the same name. What a success story! Born in Rapallo, he had been a confectioner's assistant in Genoa, a cocoa planter in Uruguay, a coffee exporter in Lima, a forty-niner in the California Gold Rush, and the founder of America's first chocolate dynasty. Grandpa learned everything he could about the Ghirardelli Company and afflicted friends and relatives with trivia. Did they know Ghirardelli employed 150 people, produced 250 tons of chocolate a year, and generated profits of $18 million? If anyone yawned, he flew into a rage. One day, he swore, he would hitchhike to San Francisco, lunch at Ghirardelli Square, and drink from a chocolate fountain. This pipe dream drove Nonna Agata crazy.

"Why don't you pay the rent instead of buying that crap?" she scolded.

"Go plant nails!" Grandpa said.

When he retired, he had no pension, thanks to spotty employment. But Grandpa was a thief as well as a goldbrick. One day Nonna and Mamma found a lump in the kitchen linoleum. It was a wad of cash. Five hundred bucks! But nobody dared to confront him. He looked as cuddly as garden troll, but when crossed he became a Tasmanian devil. He lashed out with his hands or, worse, his maimed tongue, which was sharper than an awl. His family left him alone and tolerated his grandiose tales. When he met my paternal grandfather Carlo, a fellow *menefreghista,* during the early days of my parents' courtship, he impersonated a big shot.

"Beezaness is-a beezaness, Signor Di Renzo," he said, tilting back on his chair and hitching his belt. The two bums laughed.

"A fine pair of artichokes," Nonna grumbled in the kitchen.

Grandpa let her stew. After all, he was Joseph Profaci's jester.

Every two or three months, a black Caddy would shadow Grandpa, pull to the curb, and whisk him away to Don Profaci. If these private audiences occurred at the family's three-house compound on Fifteenth Avenue, Grandpa would be home for supper. But if they took place at the don's hunting lodge in Etra, New Jersey, formerly belonging to Teddy Roosevelt, or his sprawling Long Island estate, Grandpa could be gone for days. Don Profaci always pretended it was a social call, but everyone knew it was a command performance.

With his dark hornrims, pencil moustache, and slight jowls, Joseph Profaci resembled a high-school math teacher, but he was cruel and vindictive, despite a reputation for piety. The don kept an altar in his basement. His face appeared in a mural of the Assumption on the ceiling of Regina Pacis. For his generous donations to Catholic charities, leading clerics had petitioned Pope Pius XII to confer a knighthood; the Vatican would have complied if Brooklyn DA Miles McDonald had not protested. But when a punk had the temerity to steal a jeweled crown from the Madonna at St. Bernadette, where Profaci and Grandpa were communicants, the don felt personally insulted. Blood would flow, he warned, unless someone made amends. No fence dared to handle the jewels, so the crown was returned. Nevertheless, Profaci still ordered a hit. The young thief was strangled with a rosary, chopped to pieces, and dumped in the East River.

Because the Sicilian black market supplied Don Profaci with Bonajuto chocolate, the old dragon always lured Grandpa into his lair. He played the kindly host, the wheedling *paisan.* "Play for me, Menico. Something light," he would say, and Grandpa obliged with "'*A Casciaforte*" or "*O Spuorto 'e Mulberry Stritto.*" Don Profaci shook with laughter. He desperately needed cheering up, for his world was fraying. The Kefauver hearings had focused a media spotlight on the Mafia, and Profaci's arrest at the Apalachin conference had exposed his family and fomented a rebellion. The Gallo brothers had started a civil war, backed by Carlo Gambino, Vito Genovese, and Tommy Lucchese. Each day, Profaci's power ebbed. Cornered and betrayed, he howled at fate as Grandpa strummed his mandolin and ate chocolate.

Lear and his fool.

The two Villabatesi declined together. Don Profaci battled cancer. Grandpa contracted diabetes but continued his chocolate binges, even after his toes were amputated. He single-mindedly pursued death like a once-in-a-lifetime business opportunity. Shrunken and toothless, he would rock and suck caramels beneath the sycamore in front of his duplex, his eyes closed, humming a lullaby. If you can't be a god, you might as well be an infant. That was the logic of his Sicilian death wish. As Prince Fabrizio observes in Lampedusa's *The Leopard:* "All Sicilian expression, even the most violent, is really wish-fulfillment: our sensuality is a hankering for

oblivion, our shooting and knifing a hankering for death; our lazi-
ness, our spiced and drugged sherbets, a hankering for voluptuous
immobility, that is, for death again." That was why Grandpa main-
lined Ghirardelli.

Mamma, the baby of the family, tried to save him. But when
she chained the refrigerator door to keep him from sneaking
food, he rewarded her with language that would have shamed a
Hell's Kitchen junkman. A moocher to the end, Grandpa refused
to shell out the five bucks per insulin shot. Instead, Mamma had
to drag him to Coney Island Hospital and used her pin money to
pay for his meds. My father finally put his foot down. One day, as
Papa carried him upstairs after another stressful hospital visit,
Grandpa went on a tear. Papa stopped, fixed him in the eye, and
said as calmly as if he were reading a bus schedule: "Old man, if I
chucked you down these stairs, no one would give a damn."

Grandpa shut up.

DOMENICO BILO DIED on July 27, 1964, three years after his
feudal lord Joseph Profaci. The wake was held at Andrea Terra-
grossa's Funeral Parlor on 1305 Seventy-ninth Street. Because St.
Bernadette was double-booked, the funeral was held at Our Lady
of Guadalupe. He is buried in St. Charles Cemetery, Long Island,
Section 23, but the double tombstone is incomplete. Nonna Agata
refused to join him in death and is buried at Pine Lawn, ten miles
away.

Don Profaci rests in St. John's Cemetery, Queens, the Mafia's
Boot Hill, entombed in a white granite, domed mausoleum,
behind two huge brass doors depicting the crucified Christ
attended by two angels. A statue of St. Aloysius, clutching a skull,
perches on the dome.

Grandpa's open grave was less impressive. "Jesus Christ," Papa
muttered. "You shoot for the sky, and you land in a hole." As the
plywood casket sank into the earth, I strewed a handful of Hershey's Kisses.

Sweets to the sweet.

CAFFÈ

*Neapolitan
Espresso*

*Coffeehouse
Philosophy*

NEAPOLITAN
ESPRESSO

SNOBS SPEND HUNDREDS, sometimes thousands, of dollars on industrial-sized espresso machines suitable for restaurants and bars. Eduardo De Fillipo, the Neaoplitan actor and playwright, would have been appalled. Anyone can prepare good *caffè* with a moka—an ordinary aluminum espresso pot.

Using steam pressure, a moka forces water through a strainer to create espresso. Bialetti, which invented this device in 1933, still sells the best and least expensive mokas. A two-cup model will produce espresso superior to the boiled ink served in most coffee houses, for less money than the hundred dollar knock-offs at Wal-Mart.

Here's how to make espresso the Neapolitan way.

MATERIALS AND INGREDIENTS
- Ground espresso beans (popular Italian brands are Illy and Kimbo)
- Sugar
- Distilled cold water
- Two-cup moka espresso pot
- Small mixing bowl
- Four ceramic demitasse cups

DIRECTIONS
1. Pour water into base of moka but do not pass fill line. If water seeps through the strainer when you insert it, the coffee will be thin and weak.
2. Fill strainer with espresso and wipe off excess grounds before assembling the pot. Form a perfect seal or water will spurt out once it boils.
   Warning: Never pack strainer! You will clog the system, build too much pressure, and turn your kitchen into a

set from *The Last Days of Pompeii*. For the best results, the espresso should lie flush with the pot's upper strainer.

3. Assemble moka. Once again, ensure no grounds form on the outside rim. Screw the pot onto base by holding the pot itself, not the handle.

4. Place moka over low heat. The longer the brew time, the richer the flavor. A slow trickle is better than a jet fountain.

5. As the espresso brews, add sugar to the mixing bowl. Start with a teaspoon per cup and then adjust to suit your taste.

6. *This critical step takes practice.* When the espresso begins to bubble out, remove pot from heat. Pour liquid slowly into the bowl and stir until the blended sugar and coffee are as thick as peanut butter. If mixture is too dry, add more espresso a little at a time until the consistency is right.

   Tip: If you run out of espresso, return pot to heat until more comes out. But the first coffee is best because it is the strongest. If you add too much espresso, you can: (a) compensate with more sugar (not recommended for diabetics), or (b) admit defeat and pour in the remaining pot. You will lose the foam but save the brew.

7. When espresso finishes brewing, pour half into bowl. Stir vigorously to aerate mixture and to produce a thick foam. The amount of foam depends on technique and the amount of sugar used. Once thoroughly mixed, add the remaining espresso to the container and mix once again.

8. Pour espresso into ceramic demitasse cups. If necessary, spoon foam. Since the cups are small, the espresso may quickly turn cold. To prevent this problem, place cups in hot water before you start brewing. Once warmed, the cups will retain the coffee's heat and allow you to serve piping hot espresso to your guests.

American supermarkets stock the most popular commercial brands of Italian espresso: Illy, Kimbo, Lavazza, Medaglia d'Oro. But coffee shops contain hidden treasures. My local Gimme Coffee, for instance, sells Piccolo Mondo Fair Trade Organic Blend.

Whatever your preference or budget, don't deny yourself the joy of making stovetop espresso. As Eduardo De Fillipo observed: "The only real cost is personal skill and patience."

COFFEEHOUSE
PHILOSOPHY

"THE DRINK OF PHILOSOPHERS," Uncle Tonino declared, sniffing his espresso. His refined but saturnine face—like the actor José Ferrer's, only puffier from overwork—was so suffused with pleasure that the *barista* behind the zinc counter half grinned. My uncle and I had spent an entire Saturday sightseeing in Rome ("Ruins and fools," Tonino had commented; "what could me more instructive?") and had ended our tour of the Eternal City at this small coffeehouse by the Pantheon.

The establishment had nothing to recommend it aesthetically, a shoddy affair of chrome, chipped marble, and secondhand Art Deco posters. But Uncle Tonino had insisted on coming here. The Pantheon district, he maintained, serves the best espresso in the city because all its cafés use *Aqua Virgo,* the soft Virgin Water flowing from the fabled Aqueduct of Agrippa. Here, he explained, one drank classicism, not coffee.

My uncle certainly seemed as poised as Horace, hovering over his demitasse. Slowly, he swirled the *crema*, the ambrosial, caramel-colored residue that forms on the surface of all good espresso, stirred in sugar to spite his doctor's warnings about diabetes, and savored his coffee. "*Ahhhhhhhhhhhhh,*" he said. His customary melancholy faded away, and for a moment he was content, even beatific, his face wreathed by a nimbus of steam. "That reconciles a man to his life," he remarked, then leaned forward and added confidentially: "As I said, my boy, I am a coffeehouse philosopher."

At the time, I thought he simply meant he was a man of the world. Now that I myself have become something of a coffeehouse philosopher, straining the grinds of failure from the cup of my own life, I know better. A coffeehouse philosopher is more sage than *bon vivant,* a connoisseur of irony and disappointment who prefers taking life strong and black. Socrates in prison quaffed his hemlock in one gulp. But a coffeehouse philosopher sips his poison little by little in public over a lifetime. He drinks what is bitter without bitterness and dies in an odor of espresso.

If anyone had the credentials to be a coffeehouse philosopher, it was Uncle Tonino. Urbane, detached, and adaptable, he was a man equally at home in the past and the present, someone who equally appreciated a Piranesi etching of the Forum and an Armando Testa poster for Paulista Coffee. Forums and coffee, in fact, defined his life.

A business journalist and advertising executive, my uncle had covered or handled such major coffee firms as Lavazza, Classico Caffè Circi, and Illycaffè. He once boasted that he was the only man in Rome who knew both the exact number of saints atop Bernini's colonnade at St. Peter's (284) and the exact number of espresso cups made daily at the Nuova Point china factory (15,000). Tonino began his career as a provincial surveyor, spending the better part of his youth traversing the Abruzzi with transit, tripod, compass, and paper. Following World War II, however, he dreamed of becoming another Luigi Barzini, so he journeyed to America to work as an announcer at one of New York's two Italian American radio stations.

Manhattan exhilarated him with its skyscrapers, subways, and billboards. After the rubble of the war, America seemed as prosperous as Augustan Rome, and my uncle took the same pleasure charting the trajectory of the postwar boom as he had mapping the peaks of the Apennines. He liked American cars, American clothes, American movie stars. The only thing he disliked was American coffee. "Rocket fuel," he called it. He mocked people standing in line at the Chock Full o' Nuts cafeteria, upbraided my father for investing money in Maxwell House, spat in batches of percolated coffee. Until he died, his nose wrinkled whenever anyone mentioned Nescafé.

This *bête noire*, notwithstanding, he remained an unapologetic, if critical, lover of America until McDonald's opened a restaurant in the Piazza di Spagna and served instant espresso in Styrofoam cups. Then he raged like a madman at the swindles of time and the grotesqueries of globalization. But even on the worst days, when his Pirandellian tirades cowed his wife and exasperated his cronies, he always savored a strong cup of coffee and showed a wry affection towards the foolish American nephew who bears his name.

The hard-bitten *barista*, a pug in a soiled apron, beamed at us approvingly—until he noticed and scowled at the glass of milk in my hand. This was during my wholesome phase, a period of madness that lasted between my fourteenth and twenty-sixth year, during which I impersonated Mr. Rogers. If you can imagine a young Al Pacino wearing turtlenecks, cardigans, and Hush Puppies, that was me. I was clean. I was earnest. I was credulous. I was as kind and as priggish as a Methodist missionary. I had more hopes in my belly than Pandora's box, and I used words like God and democracy, peace and justice the way certain Long Island matrons use overdrawn credit cards. "So good he's good for nothing" was Tonino's judgment.

The *barista* also had me pegged: *un astèmio,* a goddamn teetotaler! He bristled with contempt. I could see his lower lip curl. So did Uncle Tonino, who, to help me save face, took a teaspoon of espresso and placed it in my milk. The dark stain transformed my goody-goody drink ("Seventeen years old and you still drink milk!") into elegant *latte macchiato.* This libation appeased the *barista,* whose rising anger subsided into a cynical shrug. "*Meno male,*" he said. Not bad. I sat there, flabbergasted, while Tonino sipped his coffee.

"How's your milk?" he asked in English. His tone was malicious, his face impassive, and he never raised his eyes from the cup.

"Ruined," I said. "Why did you put coffee in it?"

He arched an eyebrow. "A reminder," he said.

The *barista* huffily began grinding coffee beans. The noise startled me, and Uncle Tonino smiled acridly. "Do you know that sonnet by Giuseppe Belli," he asked, "'The Coffeehouse Philosopher'?" I shook my head, and he began reciting in the Romanesco dialect: "*L'ommini de sto monno só ll'istesso / Che vvaghi de caffè nner mascinino . . .*" Men in this life are just like coffee beans going into an espresso machine. First one, then another, a steady stream, all of them heading for the same fate. Round and round they go, always changing places, and often the big bean crushes the little bean. But they've hardly begun when they crowd each other through that iron door and are crushed into powder. And that's the way people live: soft or hard, mixed together by the hand of fate, which stirs them round and round in circles; and gently or roughly, everyone moves, draws breath, without ever understanding why, then cascades down the throat of death.

Belli's sonnet has since become one of my favorite poems. In fact, I consider it a personal present, since Belli composed it on my birthday, January 22, 1836. But when I first heard it, it appalled me. I was an innocent at the time, and my face must have turned as white as my milk. Defensively, I attributed this shock tactic to my uncle's morbidity. Despite his many accomplishments, his life always has been shadowed by a terrible disappointment: the death of his first-born son, Carlo, which cut short his ambitions in America and forced him to return to Italy. Whenever he finished his espresso, his eyes lingered at the bottom of the cup as if searching for something lost, as if coffee grinds and the dust of the dead were the same thing. I thought of the cup-shaped funeral urns in Rome's underground columbaria and shuddered. Uncle Tonino saw I was shaken but merely asked: "Why don't you drink coffee anymore?"

"*Scusi?*"

"*Caffè*," he said. "You loved it as a boy. Why don't you drink it anymore?"

His tone, so earnest, so heartsick, so reproachful, gave me pause. But I had been brainwashed by enough suburban YMCA lectures to reply: "Well, it's not good for you."

At this Tonino threw up his hands in exasperation. "Jackass!" he said. "And since when is life about what's good for you?!"

THAT KOAN WAS THE beginning of my enlightenment, my initiation into the Society of Coffeehouse Philosophers. It has taken me twenty years and thousands of demitasses simply to reach the postulancy of this ancient Italian order. But as the Zen masters say, "Practice is endless." I still have a lifetime to go. The Society of Coffeehouse Philosophers may not be as old or as venerable as the Knights of Malta, but its aims are just as laudable—to cultivate intelligence, irony, and wit in the dull and the naïve, and to safeguard reason, maturity, and taste in a world that is rapidly becoming a psychotic amusement park. To accomplish these goals, the

Society offers its members these three guiding principles, somewhat corresponding to Buddha's Four Noble Truths: *honor the past without illusion, live in the present without complacency, embrace the future without hope.*

This creed is secular in the best sense of the word. The Society of Coffeehouse Philosophers promises neither salvation nor nirvana. It will not deliver you from absurdity, forgive your sins, or provide a pacifier for your Inner Child. Any evangelist or New Age quack can point the way to heaven. It takes a true philosopher to teach you how to behave in the piazza and to drink your espresso. Coffeehouse philosophy sees society, for all its faults, as necessary and pleasurable, accepts human beings as beanbags of contradiction that no ideology can explain, values nature but places a premium on manners, accepts technology but never succumbs to utopianism. And like all philosophies, it deals with morality and mortality, teaching its adherents to live well in order to die well.

Those who follow this path have a shot at becoming sane, robust, civilized adults. Those who do not risk insipidness or madness. That's how bad our civilization has become. Daily, we see lovers and relatives, friends and colleagues, acquaintances and strangers forfeit their humanity. Verily, verily, I say unto thee: if you do not eat *biscotti* and drink espresso, you could devolve into a couch potato, dance an S & M *pas de deux* with every telemarketer who interrupts your TV dinner, prowl bulk warehouses to get deep discounts on junk food, join health spas, shopper's clubs, and ashrams in a vain attempt to exorcise the emptiness and mediocrity devouring your soul, discuss your sex life in excruciating detail on *Jenny Jones,* surrender your sanity and life savings to Oral Roberts, massacre dozens of people with an Uzi because you were shortchanged a Chicken McNugget. The choice is becoming increasingly clear: either the espresso cup of wisdom or the Kool-Aid pitcher of Jonestown.

Accordingly, to promote and preserve the public good, I have decided to violate one of the most important rules of coffeehouse philosophy—not to preach in public without a newspaper or a *cappuccino*—to discuss its history, practices, and beliefs and their impact on my life. Before I reveal these Masonic secrets, however, you must swear by the Grand Sultans Pope, Goldoni, and Voltaire, by the Exalted Viziers Pavoni, Illy, and Gaggia, never to reveal what I am about to tell you to the foolish, the gross, or the boring, especially to those Seattle yuppies who treat coffee like liquid potpourri. If you break this oath, may your pantry never hold anything but Sanka, may your blood turn into Folgers' crystals, may you be bound like Ixion on a Williams Sonoma coffee grinder!

BEFORE THERE WAS coffeehouse philosophy, there was coffee. The first shipment of arabica arrived in Venice from Constantinople in 1615. Coffee was a relative latecomer to Italy, reaching the peninsula some five years after tea and nearly a century after cocoa had been imported from the New World. Venetian merchants, however, made up for lost time through aggressive promotion. Like their predecessor, Marco Polo, and their successors, Milanese and Madison Avenue copywriters, they capitalized on their product's exoticism. With the help of musicians and *commedia dell'arte* street performers, they staged colorful skits about the origins of coffee in the Piazza di San Marco.

Two centuries earlier, a Yemen goatherd had discovered his flock munching the bright red berries of the kaffar bush. According to legend, the Queen of Sheba had brought this plant to the Middle East from Abyssinia as a wedding gift to King Solomon. The berries must have been magical, because the goats twitched their ears, bleated, and began cavorting around the bush. Fascinated, the goatherd tried some himself and joined the romp. A passing imam was struck by this interspecies break dance and secreted some berries back to his mosque. After boiling them, he roasted the pits, which he then crushed and mixed with water to form a paste. The bitter but delectable concoction proved a marvelous stimulant. The imam found he could meditate tirelessly for hours, read the Koran with greater clarity, and he decided to share the drink with his fellow muslims. Holy men prayed till dawn. Dervishes spun faster and longer. Pilgrims fortified themselves on their way to Mecca. The devout called the new beverage *kawah*, Arabic for "inspiration" or "enthusiasm"; others called it *kaffa*, after the Queen of Sheba's plant. The Italians decided to call it *caffè*.

Initially, the new drink was regarded—with good reason—as a drug, and as such it commanded a great price. A single cup cost a week's wages and could be drunk only under the supervision of a physician or an apothecary. Soon, however, lemonade vendors began selling coffee throughout Venice. Police records show that city officials regarded these vendors with suspicion. Like enterprising coke dealers, they probably cut their product to meet street, er, canal value. Ecclesiastical authorities were no less wary. The Inquisition investigated coffee merchants and expressed its concern to the Vatican. In Rome theologians wrote denunciatory tracts calling coffee "the bitter invention of Satan." Fortunately, Pope Clement VIII, a sane and intelligent man, decided to sample this witch's brew himself. One sip convinced him that he had found paradise. "Coffee," he pronounced, smacking his lips, "should be baptized to make it a true Christian drink." Some of the denser cardinals thought the pope had suggested actually baptizing infants in coffee, but they finally caught on when His Holiness boiled them a fresh pot.

The pope's imprimatur mollified the Venetian government, and over the next thirty years, *botteghe del caffè*, the first genuine coffeehouses, opened their doors. Most of these had grandiloquent names to attract customers: Duc di Toscania, Imperatore Imperatrice della Russia, Tamerlano, Fantae di Diana, Dame Venete, Arabo-Piastrelle. Caffè Florian, founded in 1683, remains Europe's oldest surviving coffeehouse, as well as its most prestigious and most expensive. It is still located in Piazza di San Marco. Unlike their counterparts in Mecca and Constantinople, these Italian cafés were not associated with religious observance. If anything, their license seemed to threaten public morals. According to contemporary chroniclers, they "tore men away from church and home." Even in this profane setting, however, coffee drinking was still a holy ritual. For the Arabs, coffee had symbolized contemplation and mystic rapture. For the emerging Society of Coffeehouse Philosophers, coffee would represent another kind of Enlightenment.

The Italian coffeehouse reached its zenith as a cultural and social institution in the eighteenth century, as apotheosized in Carlo Goldoni's 1750 comedy, *La Bottega di Caffè*. By 1763, there were over two hundred coffeehouses in Venice alone, with hundreds of others scattered throughout the peninsula as well as abroad. As early as the 1690s, in fact, Italians had begun exporting coffeehouses with the same enthusiasm Americans would export McDonald's franchises. Entrepreneurs like Pasquale Rosée helped to establish some of London's most famous coffeehouses, places like Button's, Will's, Lloyd's, each of which attracted a specific coterie of businessmen, scientists, and artists. These Italian-style cafés became known as "penny universities," because for one pence, the price of a cup of coffee, ordinary people could eavesdrop on the greatest minds of their day.

As precursors of newspapers and advertising agencies, coffeehouses encouraged writing. Dryden and Congreve, Addison and Steele, Sheridan and Goldsmith, all held court at their respective cafés. Consequently, coffee became the sacramental wine of wit, both in London and in Paris, the cultural capitals of their day, and the English satirists and the French *philosophes* drank it for health and stamina. Voltaire slurped forty to fifty cups a day, much to the despair of his doctors, who predicted he would die prematurely. (In fact, he lived to be eighty-three.) Pope cured his agonizing migraines, caused by a twisted back, by breathing coffee fumes from a vaporizer. But coffee inspired as well as sustained. Its powerful chemistry stirred debate.

"Coffee is prepared in such a way that it makes those who drink it witty," Montesquieu observed: "at least there is not a single soul who, on quitting a coffee house, does not believe himself four times wittier than when he entered it." And four times more belligerent. At the Café Procope in Saint-Germain, Montesquieu once observed a group of Parisian intellectuals argue for three hours about the *Iliad*. Both sides spoke with such fierce conviction, traded such ferocious insults, that Montesquieu expected them to brawl. But they didn't, *mirabile dictu*, unlike the seminarians in the nearby Latin Quarter, who routinely came to blows over theology.

Coffee was divine war. Spilling ink, not blood, it shook the sky or at least the Murano ceiling with Olympian laughter. Coffee tapped aggression without licensing barbarism, which explains why the era's greatest wits—Swift, who blandly advocated cannibalism and infanticide to denounce starvation in Ireland; Diderot, who joked that "man will never be free until the last king is strangled with the entrails of the last priest"—were so stark, raving sane. By reconciling the superego and id, coffee formed a harmonious partnership worthy of Mozart and Da Ponte.

The Romantics later dismissed the Enlightenment as the cold Age of Reason, but never again would civilized people be more honestly or passionately in touch with their outrage. Coffeehouses considered anger a gentleman's prerogative, a sign of rationality and grace, provided it was refined enough. If this policy seems self-serving, consider the following passage from Aristotle's *Nicomachean Ethics*: "A person who is angry at the right things and towards the right people, in the right way, at the right moment, and for the right length of time, should be praised. Such a person is truly mild, for genuine mildness means being not easily disturbed by feelings, but irritated at whatever reason prescribes and for the length of time it prescribes it."

In other words, a cultivated contempt keeps society sane because it vaccinates citizens against delusion and mania. Tolerate anything, and you start believing alien abduction groupies and allegations of Satanic ritual abuse. Of all the insights of the Enlightenment, those formed in the coffeehouse are perhaps the most precious. Put succinctly, *every human being has the God-given right to be sarcastic, and should gratefully pay for that right by being the willing butt of others if his or her own foolishness merits it.* Without this necessary dialectic between civility and hostility, citizens will become either too wimpy or too savage for their own good, either will waste their lives in a Christian Science Reading Room or waste someone else in a drive-by shooting. That principle is the cornerstone of coffeehouse philosophy.

Such stimulating thinking was hardly limited to England and France, of course. Italy, too, had splendid coffeehouses, many of which are still in business and have become beloved landmarks, such as the Caffè Florian in Padua, Stendhal's favorite haunt, and the Caffè degli Specchi in Trieste, whose decor of gilded mirrors proves conclusively that coffeehouses were a place of reflection. There was much to think about. Italy in the eighteenth century was a miserable place, neither an actual country nor a profitable tourist trap. Goldoni's Venice had gone to pot, dissipating its financial and political capital on courtesans and masquerades. Rome was a backwater of malarial swamps and unshaven prelates. Ruins of the glorious past seemed a hollow mockery. Poverty, or the threat of it, was epidemic, and people became *virtuosi* of deceit, conning, scalping, conniving, just to put bread on the table.

In this atmosphere of bankruptcy and oppression, charlatanism and grotesquery, the coffeehouse became a place of refuge. Where else could a sane person go? Catholicism had become discredited, and the opera had become dominated by claques and *castrati*. Only at the coffeehouse could one express oneself freely, without fear of confessor, policeman, or in-laws. It was the Great Good Place. When the pompous, back-biting Don Marzio is expelled from the coffeehouse at the end of *La Bottega del Caffè*, he laments that he has lost his soul. He was not exaggerating. Coffeehouses provided the kind of order and balance, security and dignity that make life bearable and civilized. They humanized the monstrous.

Nowhere was this more necessary than in the abject South, which had been colonized by the Bourbons. To compensate, Naples developed phenomenal coffeehouses. They used only the purest water, roasted their coffee beans to produce the richest, darkest blend in Europe. They also pioneered *al fresco* seating. Coffee drinkers could loll outside and contemplate Mount Vesuvius, smoldering in the distance, could discuss the ongoing excavations at Pompeii and bet on the next eruption. Significantly, one of the earliest and most popular espresso machines, a small metal boiler called *la macchinetta napolitana*, was a miniature Vesuvius—a reminder to espresso lovers that disaster lurks in the middle of domesticity, but that even in the shadow of squalor and extermination one can achieve serenity and contentment.

ESPRESSO ITSELF IS A product of the Industrial Revolution, of the more technical side of the Enlightenment. When Giovanni Battista Beccaria in the 1770s began lecturing on the recently patented Watt steam engine, eccentric and enterprising *baristas* began using steam power to boil coffee. But it wasn't until the 1840s that a Scottish inventor, Robert Napier, first developed a method of vacuum-brewing coffee. Napier's experiments inspired Italian scientists to use stream pressure to force water through ground coffee in a filter, and within a decade, the prototype for the stovetop espresso machine had been invented. That didn't satisfy the *baristas*, though. They wanted a brewing method that would jet-propel water through ground coffee, a streamlined process that would extract the oily quintessence of the beans without any bitterness.

By the turn of the century, the first true espresso machines made their sibilant debut in Milan. These were upright metal urns, not unlike high-tech Russian samovars, with gauges and handles. The latter allowed boiling water and steam to be channeled to spigots with replaceable filters full of grinds. The pressure forced, or expressed, the water and steam through the filter to create the coffee—hence the term *caffè espresso*. *Espresso* was already a colloquial restaurant term that meant "made to order." But the word had other nuances that also seemed fitting. Drinking the new coffee gave you a rush, a sense of speed, like being on an express train. Thoughts came to you more quickly, as if through express mail. You found yourself more talkative, more willing to express yourself. Even your face became more expressive. *Espresso!* It was fuel-injection, Bergson's *élan vital,* champagne and gasoline—the perfect drink for the twentieth century!

While Marinetti and the Futurists praised the new elixir, Italian scientists rushed to improve the espresso machine with the same determination with which American scientists would hasten to put a man on the moon. What followed was a mock heroic epic worthy of Pope, or at least a doctoral dissertation at the Rennsaeler Polytechnic Institute.

Trailblazer Desiderio Pavoni in 1907 patented a contraption that could make a hundred and fifty cups of coffee an hour. Just two years later, Teresio Arduino introduced the mother of all espresso machines, the classic Victoria Arduino, with an astonishing capacity of a thousand cups an hour. The Victoria Arduino is the espresso machine of my grandparents' generation. A brass tabernacle surmounted by Jove's eagle, it poured liquid thunder for its worshippers. Immigrants brought the Arduino to these shores and installed them in coffeehouses in every major Little Italy. Customs and licensing were never a problem because the inspectors were convinced that the spread eagle honored America: "Downright patriotic of you, Gooseppy!"

Although many Italian American coffeehouses, for nostalgic reasons, still use these functioning antiques, the Arduino is only the Model T of espresso technology. In 1936 Francisco Illy, a

Triestan chemist and technician, substituted compressed air for steam, producing the first automatic espresso machine. After World War Two, Achilles Gaggia introduced a hand-lever mechanical piston to replace steam pressure. His refinement produced a fast, high-pressure extraction, characterized by a thick layer of foam or *crema,* which set a new standard for espresso brewing. By the time Ernesto Valente in 1961 had replaced the spring lever with a rotating pump driven by a small electric motor, the espresso machine had become more compact and efficient, and espresso itself smoother and cleaner.

Given this technology, a good *barista* must be an engineer, a physicist, and a chemist. He must tamp down 7 grams of extremely fine-ground coffee with a force of 50 pounds per square inch and then shoot an ounce of fresh, hot water (192 to 198 degrees F) through the grind with a force of about 130 psi: all within a time span of 18 to 24 seconds. His scientific method are the Four M's: *macinazione* (the correct grinding of the coffee blend), *miscela* (the "mix" of the blend), *macchina* (the espresso machine), *mano* (the skilled hand of the operator). Any step can be fatally compromised. Beans must be ground to the right consistency—fine but not pulverized. The texture of table salt, ideally. If the grind is too coarse, the coffee will gush out thin and watery; if it is too fine, the coffee will drip too slowly and be bitter. The same balance must be achieved in the roast itself. If the coffee is too light or too dark, it will taste respectively like lemonade or creosote.

Then there is the problem of pressure. Good espresso pressure must be both functional and aesthetically pleasing, must hold and reconcile tensions in equilibrium like a heroic couplet. If the beans are tamped too loosely, water will flood the chamber; too tightly, and nothing can get through. The telltale sign is the *crema,* which should be evenly colored and as much as a quarter-inch thick. As you drink, it should coat the side of your cup like syrup. A dark brown *crema* with a white dot or black hole in the middle signifies that the espresso has been over-extracted and will taste harsh and bitter. A light brown *crema,* on the other hand, indicates an under-extracted espresso that will taste weak.

Considering these obstacles, every good cup of espresso is a triumph of science and the human spirit; and a good *barista,* to stay in business, must consistently achieve excellence—sometimes making as many as ten thousand cups of espresso a day.

If this digression reads like a parody of NASA ("Houston, we have *crema* . . ."), it points to a central concern of coffeehouse philosophy—the role of technology in human affairs. And by technology, I don't just mean machinery but all the tools with which human beings fashion themselves: language, art, manners, customs. In short, the software of culture. Coffeehouse philosophers may be traditionalists, but they are not Luddites. How could they be, when espresso brewing is such an exact science? They concede that our humanity is more a matter of technique than nature. But they insist that technology should enhance, not diminish, human happiness and wisdom. Nothing could be more antithetical to the life-crushing spirit of American techno-capitalism.

"Italians," said Uncle Tonino, "treat coffee machines like people. Americans treat people like coffee machines."

We sat at the espresso bar near the Pantheon, observing the tourists. Tonino was on a roll. Mr. Coffee, the automatic drip machine, which had been released in the United States some five years earlier, capturing 60 percent of the market, had been introduced in Italy and was shockingly gaining ground. Tonino was beside himself. He rolled his eyes, flared his nostrils. The veins in his temples bulged, and his teeth gnashed as if they were crushing pistachios. "The bastard should be hung by his heels like Mussolini!"

He was alluding to Vincent G. Marotta, the Italian American entrepreneur who had invented Mr. Coffee. A real-estate developer and self-styled inventor, he had substituted the Four M's of espresso brewing with the Two D's of percolation: *drip* and *dreck*. His first unit, the CM-1, had conquered America, thanks to high saturation advertising. Marotta, a former athlete, who had outfielded for the St. Louis Cardinals, ran first-team track as a world-class sprinter, and even played football for the Cleveland Browns, had convinced Joe DiMaggio to be his spokesperson. For Tonino, this was a double betrayal. Not only had Marotta turned his back on espresso, but he had transformed Joltin' Joe into a cup of joe, one with no jolt at all. Tonino and my father had seen DiMaggio play at Yankee Stadium, which even Tonino admitted had better bleachers than the Coliseum, and he was shaken to see the

Clipper act in those commercials. The insurance-salesman delivery, the aw-shucks smile, the trustworthy glint in the eye, he was like a Disneyland automaton.

"It's the coffee," Tonino insisted. "Percolated coffee corrodes the soul. Do you know where your famous American coffee break comes from? The war. During World War Two, when the factories ran all night making bombs and planes and tanks, the big shots, the *pescicani*, noticed people worked longer, faster, better, if they kept some coffee handy. After the war, corporations took up the practice. Tanks and planes, cars and washing machines: what was the difference? Two American G.I.s had invented the automatic coffee machine. Filters were already available. That German woman, that Melitta what's-her-name, Benz, had made them. Used blotting paper from her son's writing desk. Melitta Coffee. She was from Dresden. I guess the Americans roasted her beans when they firebombed the city. But that machine. It made everything easy. You didn't have to be there. You didn't have to think. You didn't have to care. Just let it drip down, settle on the bottom, and burn. It scalded your tongue, numbed your brain. *Ahi, ahi!* Poor Joe. Wasn't it bad enough he married La Monroe?"

I weighed my uncle's words carefully, considered how much drip coffee had upset him, saw the stricken expression on the *barista*'s pug face. Then I heard myself say in Italian: "That's not a coffee machine, goddamn it. That's a fucking cistern."

The *barista* gaped in disbelief, but Uncle Tonino, stroking his chin, looked pleased. "Antonio," he said, "there's hope for you yet."

OVER THE YEARS, I have clung to these words, hoping that one day—despite my foolishness—I too may become a coffeehouse philosopher like my uncle. According to my parents, I once had great potential. As a toddler, I seemed destined for the coffeehouse. Throughout my early years in Brooklyn, I adored espresso, drinking two to three demitasses with every meal. Coffee was my milk, my morning hymn. Along with excerpts from *La Traviata*, I loved singing with my mother the Medaglia D'Oro jingle: "*Medaglia D'Oro é un dono / Che vale piu del'oro/Bevendo il mio caffè / Caffè Medaglia D'Oro!*" Gold Medal Coffee is a gift worth more than gold. Maybe the jingle writer remembered the words of the sixteenth-century sage, Abd-al Kadir: "Coffee is the common man's gold, and like gold it brings every man the feeling of luxury and nobility."

I needed to share this boon with others. Coffee wasn't really coffee unless I drank it in public. At home I enjoyed our little Neapolitan boiler, a Lavazza engraved with a caricature of an Eduardo De Fillipo type hoisting a steaming cup of coffee, but the day seemed empty if I didn't drink espresso from a real espresso machine. Every grocery run, every trip to the tailor, every expedition to the shoemaker in Bayridge and Bensonhurst ended at a neighborhood coffeehouse. And no trip to New York's Little Italy would be complete without a stop at Ferrara, the famous cafè on Grand Street. They had a huge dessert display, crammed with *cannoli,* honey puffs, pine nut tarts, almond paste cookies, *biscotti,* and *tiramisú.*

But I never wanted sweets. I always wanted espresso, and the stronger the better. I would take my coffee *ristretto,* short and dense, or *corretto,* with a shot of Vecchia Romagna brandy or Grappa di Julia. Often I asked for Averna, a bitter Sicilian cordial made from a two-hundred-year-old recipe of herbs and roots. Once the *barista* shook his head in disbelief. Wouldn't I prefer *espresso macchiato,* served with a tiny spot of milk? But I pounded the counter and demanded Averna. "This kid's already an old man," said the *barista,* pouring.

"My son just knows what he wants," Papa explained.

Fortified by a steady stream of rich blackness, I always knew what I wanted then. I hadn't been Americanized yet. I was bright, I was confident, I was sophisticated, and I was witty beyond my years—as the following coffeehouse anecdote will attest: One day at Ferrara, an attaché from the United Nations arrived, a brisk, self-important man with a pencil moustache and a clipped Tuscan accent. "I have just had a disastrous meal," he announced, "and I expect a redemptive cup of coffee." The usual V.I.P. arrogance. The *barista* served him a demitasse of espresso with a lemon twist. Now, although many Italian Americans drink espresso this way, this custom in Italy is strictly limited to the Deep South, a remnant from the arid days when Sicilian *baristas* were forced to clean their cups with lemon peel during droughts or disputes over water rights. For a Northerner, lemon peel in espresso is definitely gauche. The attaché frowned. "And what," he asked coldly, "is this?"

The room fell silent, and the *barista*'s cheek began to twitch.

"*Un digestivo!*" I piped. A digestive.

The coffeehouse exploded in laughter, with the adults patting my back; and the attaché smiled and graciously drank his espresso . . . without removing the peel.

Two catastrophes, however, would evict me from this caffeinated Parnassus. During a two-year sojourn in Italy, I nearly died of dysentery, and the ordeal wreaked havoc with my digestion. Never again would I be able to drink coffee so copiously, not without upsetting my bowels. When I returned to the States, my family relocated to Freehold, New Jersey, the site of a Nescafé factory. Whenever it was about to rain, the stench permeated the air and itched my skin. During the move, our beloved Lavazza had broken and could not be replaced—an ill omen, if ever there was one. I found myself marooned in a wasteland of strip malls, polyester, eight-tracks, and Hills Brothers coffee. Although my parents had bought another Neapolitan boiler from which I occasionally drank espresso, there were no Italian coffeehouses. The American family restaurants, Van's, Howard Johnson, and the completely misnamed Friendly's, didn't carry espresso and refused to serve me coffee. Uniformed waitresses would chew gum and stare daggers at my parents. "You sure this boy should drink coffee?" they slurred.

This theme was echoed in school, where teachers and administrators blamed my nervousness and sarcasm on espresso. "Mrs. Di Renzo," the monsignor explained, his wattles wobbling, "coffee isn't good for a boy with such a high-strung temperament." Actually, I had become high strung from the numerous beatings I had received at the hands of my schoolmates, due to my size, intelligence, and accent, but none of the adults seemed to see that. They compared me to the poster child in that classic C.W. Post ad, "Held Back by Coffee." Even my ethnic features—my oily hair, olive complexion, and short height, the dark circles under my eyes—were interpreted as symptoms of caffeinism. These folks meant well, but if they were really on the side of the angels, why were they haunted by the ghost of Juan Valdez?

Everyone joined the conspiracy to alienate me from espresso: PTA marms, mother superiors, gym teachers, YMCA counselors. They not only wanted to save me from espresso but from the coffeehouse itself, which represented everything they hated about Italian culture. It was decadent, pessimistic, reactionary, defeatist—just a bunch of cynics lapping poison and cracking jokes. I was too good for that, they said. I was an American boy now. Didn't I know I had a duty to keep myself mentally and morally clean? Didn't I know my body was God's temple? Those were the puritans. The boosters, the Rotarians, the Chamber of Commerce blowhards, the parish pols, and the V.F.W. foghorns, took another tack. By all means, they said, drink your coffee, provided you've earned it. But don't be morbid about it. In a healthy, functioning society, coffee is supposed to get you up in the morning. It keeps you productive and cheerful, powers the G.N.P. and propels the space program. Against such stupidity, the gods themselves are helpless. What chance did a ten-year-old boy have?

I did not go gentle into that bland night. Up until my twelfth, thirteenth year, I disputed my teachers whenever they misrepresented Italian culture and history and even smuggled *Gulliver's Travels* and *Candide* into my Confirmation class. Inevitably, though, the Boy Scout propaganda took hold. The coffee drip, the Chinese water torture, proved too much. I stopped drinking espresso, and I stopped speaking Italian. I also, not coincidentally, stopped being snide. I convinced myself that if I were less clever, less ironic, less skeptical, less impertinent, I finally would be accepted and happy. Of course, I never wholly rid myself of certain knee-jerk sarcasms any more than I could completely shed my accent. But I was determined to be nice. I checked in to the Julie Andrews Clinic, where white-coated lab technicians freeze-dried and decaffeinated me as the P.A. system played excerpts from *The Sound of Music*. Later, in high school, I enrolled in a twelve-step anti-misanthropy program, sponsored by Leo Buscaglia. Every day, I celebrated my delivery from inner darkness with three tall glasses of milk.

To be fair, some of this institutionalized lactation and detoxification was necessary, even beneficial. Bigotry and persecution had so embittered me that I had become a little gila monster. This was uncivil. True maturity requires a certain purity, after all, just as good espresso requires virgin water. But I had overcompensated. Now I was a regular Parsifal: a holy innocent, a guileless fool; and like a saint, I suffered fools gladly—no matter how stupidly or cruelly they behaved. This was immoral. It is one thing to forgive foolishness, in oneself and others; it is another thing to ignore, excuse, or condone it. I had become a threat to myself and society. Over the next ten years, I did incredible damage. Always with the kindest intentions, of course.

Fortunately, this sweet self melted in the cauldron of experience the way a sugar cube melts in a cup of java. Failure, betrayal, and neurasthenia weaned me away from milk and guided me back to espresso. I will spare you the details. Coffeehouse philosophers refuse to complain unless they can be witty. But the turning point is entertaining enough. At the wedding of a former fiancée, a wholesome American girl (a one-time dairy queen, by the way, and a distant cousin of Pat Boone's), I was mistaken for the Italian caterer in the reception line. "Where's the coffee?" asked a dumpy, florid-faced matron, wearing a hideous teal dress and an orchid corsage. "Home," I said. And I drove back to Syracuse, New York, found a coffeehouse in Little Italy, and drank ten cups of espresso at one sitting. I was on the toilet the rest of the night, but that was the beginning of my recovery.

Since then, I have turned to espresso again and again whenever life turns bitter—when office politics nearly scuttle my career; when a childless future stares me grimly in the face; when old friends end up on the street, in the asylum, or on death row, and I can do nothing to help them; when beloved students sell out to corporate headhunters or are blown up by terrorist bombs; when the written word is menaced by illiteracy and MTV executives; most especially, when another piece of Italian culture is exterminated or co-opted by the American empire. To my horror, espresso itself is rapidly becoming one such casualty. Consumerism and narcissism, the yin and yang of American capitalism, have made a coffee-table book out of coffeehouse culture. Corporations have mainstreamed the ethnic café, transforming a world of intellectual stimulation and political ferment into a world of designer catalogues and glossy magazines. The cover of a recent issue of *Coffee Journal* shows a lanky Midwestern farmer drinking Italian coffee. "HERE'S MUD IN YOUR CUP!" reads the headline. "ESPRESSO HITS THE FARM BELT!"

"That stuff really gives you a kick in the rear, and I like that!" proclaims Merrill Mawdsley of Algona, Iowa.

Now I'm all for Hawkeyes drinking espresso—provided they are not being manipulated by Northwestern marketers. Don't get me started on Seattle, the so-called Espresso Capital of America. I know all the statistics: Seattle has 450 espresso carts, 4,000 commercial espresso machines, 10,000 *baristas*. Espresso is so popular, in fact, that all kinds of businesses—museums and shopping malls, beauty parlors and fashion boutiques, hardware stores and car washes—have an espresso bar. Seattle even has drive-up espresso booths and "Espresso Dental," a dental clinic that serves espresso in its waiting room. Those folks sure must clean up. Clients can stain and whiten their teeth in one sitting. Like Microsoft, Seattle's major coffee companies are billion-dollar multinationals, interested in expanding their espresso empire for the sake of a few bean counters. To prove their power, they have coerced local dairies around Puget Sound to deliver coffee beans to home-route customers along with fresh milk.

"A coffeehouse is a place where people want to be alone, but need company to do it," said one Microserf, his spreadsheet taking up an entire table. Bullshit. A coffeehouse is where you share the treasures of your loneliness with other people. You'll have plenty of time to be alone in the grave. That is why, despite an eighty-hour work week (another blessing of late capitalism), I go out whenever I can.

When I lived in Syracuse, I avoided the grunge cafés near Marshall Street and the trendy gourmet shops on Armory Square. Instead, I visited the few remaining coffeehouses on the Italian North Side. Café Express, on the corner of Ash and Lodi streets, just a stone's throw from Squadrito's Grocery, was an aggressively masculine place with a billiard table, Sinatra posters, and satellite broadcasts of Italian soccer games. The regulars were fond of me, but we has little in common. "A little pool, *professore?*" they teased. Sometimes the fossils from the Villa Scalabrini Retirement Home doddered in, with their battered fedoras and Old World manners, and I played *briscola* and *scupa* with them. I was the only one who knew these antique card games and who could converse with them in Italian.

On Sundays, I patronized Lombardi's on Butternut and Lodi, which had a café and a *gelateria* attached to its deli and import store. But the coffeehouse closed in 1996. The wake lasted two years. Before being auctioned, those wonderful espresso machines—two Valentes, a Gaggia, and pieces of an Arduino— were covered in cloth like stiffs in a morgue, as if awaiting an autopsy of ethnicity. That left Caffè d'Italia on North Salina Street, which served exquisite Turkish coffee, thick and sludgy. Here I read the Italian paper and enjoyed the Sicilian decor: a pygmy donkey cart; a marionette of Orlando in golden armor; a terra-cotta *trinacria*. The last, a three-legged hex sign, symbolized both Sicily and Hecate Trivium, the goddess of crossroads, rubbish, and the dead. An appropriate symbol, for the café was often deserted, providing no opportunity for conversation.

In the twilight of the idols, then, I must be a philosopher without a coffeehouse. Like some Diaspora Jew after the destruction of the Temple, I perform once public rituals in private without a context. To that end, I use a little Krups espresso machine, an anniversary present from my wife. My Krups makes decent espresso, but that isn't the point anymore. I drink espresso as a way to honor my dead and to mourn the passing of my culture. It is difficult to do either without succumbing to sentimentality. The last time I was at Ferrara, an NYU graduate student entertained the patrons with traditional Neapolitan street songs. He was a fresh-scrubbed, cherub-faced mediocrity with a sandy pompadour, and he butchered such favorites as "Sorrento" and "Mattinata." In better circumstances, the audience would have booed him, but they were so blinded by nostalgia, so blissed out by pastries, that they applauded and threw money. The *barista* and I exchanged looks and rolled our eyes. "This joint's become a museum," I said. Since then, Ferrara has gone corporate and now markets instant espresso.

Needless to say, I have never returned.

"*A REMINDER*," said Uncle Tonino, as he stained my milk with coffee. A reminder of what? Of mortality, perhaps. Of the ironies of history, the inevitability of change, the death of civilizations.

Also, of that deep, dark stain that never leaves your soul. Theologians presume to call this original sin, but philosophers know it is only experience, which is bitter but delicious. That consolation, with every sip, prepares me for my own death.

Sometimes I imagine that the afterlife is an eighteenth-century coffeehouse. I have a recurring dream in which I visit a London café, and Addison and Steele, Pope and Swift, Boswell and Johnson greet me warmly. I am a Sicilian banker and man of letters, a classics lecturer at the University of Naples and a biographer of Vico, and I have written a marvelous satire on paper currency, which has just been translated into English by Smollett and is enjoying a great vogue. Drinking coffee, the wits and I discuss politics and literature, read aloud from each other's work, improvise epigrams, trade criticisms and coins. Although my English is quite good, everyone, out of respect and consideration, attempts to speak to me in Italian. It is the feast of reason and the flow of soul.

But that is wishful thinking, as perhaps this essay has been an exercise in wishful thinking. The Italian coffeehouse, for all its splendor, was a product of early capitalism. Maybe its destruction at the hands of late capitalism is an act of retribution, a bit of karma. The Arabs might have thought so—not to mention the poor barmaids, who were not always amused by those bourgeois wits. None of us can know, much less redeem, the past, just as none of us can know the afterlife. On this subject, Uncle Tonino might have quoted Belli: "*Sta cane eternitá ddev'èsse eterna!*" That bitch eternity is gonna be eternal. I do know this, though: Until I die, coffee, like ink (well . . . printer toner, actually), will always be in my veins.

Without espresso, how could I express myself?

AFTER-DINNER SPEECH

Lunch with Trimalchio

LUNCH WITH TRIMALCHIO

WHEN THE PHONE RANG at 3:00 A.M., we knew it was Rome, something disastrous enough to make Uncle Tonino ignore the six-hour time difference. Jolted awake, we braced ourselves for a car accident or a cancer diagnosis. With racing hearts, we gathered around the phone as Papa barked into the receiver: "*Pronto!*" Four thousand miles away, Tonino's voice was tinny and shrill: "Buonino!" he spluttered, using Papa's boyhood name. "The barbarians have returned!" My God, what had happened? Had a lunatic vandalized another Michelangelo? Had the Red Brigade executed another premier? Had the PLO hijacked another cruiser? Worse, moaned Tonino. A McDonald's was opening in the Piazza di Spagna!

I gasped and sank to the floor. So my boss had been right, after all. Two weeks ago, while working late at our small ad agency in North Plainfield, New Jersey, he had informed me that the Golden Arches had built its first outlet in Italy. "Maybe they'll serve McPasta," he teased. Alarmed, I phoned my uncle the next day. "Bolzano," he confirmed, speaking with the confidence of a retired business journalist. "Southern Tyrol. Lots of Austrians. They want beetroot, not relish, with their burgers! Believe me, this will never catch on."

When I conveyed these assurances, my boss shook his head and flashed a Cheshire grin. "Look," he said, counting his fingers, "they've conquered Germany, they've conquered Japan, so why shouldn't they conquer Italy? You the only former Axis Power stronger than the Big Mac? Bullshit. They'll be in Rome before the end of the year. Right in the Forum."

His smugness infuriated me. "Impossible!" I blurted. "The monuments, the zoning—!"

"They'll get around it," he purred. "They always do. You can't stop progress."

Quivering, I stood and faced him. "No hamburger chain will ever capture Rome!" I said. "The Capitoline geese will prevent it!" My accent had become incomprehensible, so the boss asked me to repeat the challenge and to explain the reference. When Rome was abandoned to invading Gauls, a hilltop garrison was warned of intruders by the geese squawking in the Temple of Juno. Though deprived of food, the soldiers had rather starved than eat these sacred birds.

The boss was unimpressed. "They can squawk all they want," he said. "Those geese will be ground into Chicken McNuggets."

Indeed, they had. *Povero zio.*

Papa blistered Tonino's ear with profanity. Was this his idea of a fucking joke? I calmed Papa, pried the receiver from his hand, and consoled my uncle, who sounded as if he had been kicked in the gut. After he recovered, I asked how McDonald's had bypassed the Ufficio Speciale per gli Interventi sul Centro Storico (USICS), the Special Office for the Management of Rome's Historic Center. Diplomacy, Tonino replied. The architects from the Oak Grove, Illinois, headquarters had designed a more subdued façade and had set new standards for interior décor. Toninio had seen the prototype at the city council meeting.

· Some fine Italian hand must have suggested the winning touches. The paneled walls were made of olive wood and ceramic tile. The salad bar was bigger than a gondola and included *puntarella,* Rome's native strand of wild chicory, whose twisted wiry shoots resemble Bernini's Baldacchino in St. Peter's. The same photographer who had taken John Paul XXIII's picture for *Life,* it was noted, had done the bronze-framed portrait of McDonald's founder Ray Kroc. Prompted by the Holy Father's memory, the politicians, businessmen, and spectators applauded, drowning out objections from the city planners, engineers, and historians. The ribbon-cutting would occur in four months.

Flabbergasted, Tonino studied Ray Kroc's triumphant face, the face of a bully and a vulgarian. This hamburger king should have been cast as Trimlachio in Fellini's *Satyricon,* not Mario Romagnoli, the proprietor of Tonino's favorite *trattoria* Al Moro. Located near the Trevi Fountain, it served the best spaghetti carbonara. After the zoning fiasco, Tonino got drunk there.

"Kroc," he muttered. "What kind of name is that? Doesn't it mean 'liar'?"

"That's *crook*," I corrected.

"No, no, no! When Americans accuse someone of lying, they say, 'That's a Kroc!'"

"You're thinking of *crock*. C-r-o-c-k. Broken crockery. If a claim can't hold water—"

"It's a crock. Exactly!" pounced Tonino. "This Kroc is a liar!"

"*Zio*," I admonished, "that's just a coincidence." Actually, I wasn't entirely sure, but Papa was gesticulating for me to get off the phone. Tonino couldn't afford the long distance.

"And to think," Tonino groaned, "I used to love hamburgers!"

Zio exaggerated. Working in postwar Manhattan, he often found American hamburgers too heavy and greasy. He much preferred my mother's, which were closer to meatballs and mixed with minced onions, parsley, breadcrumbs, grated cheese, and egg yolk. But sometimes—if he needed a quick bite or wanted to learn more about his adopted country—nothing satisfied him more than a medium-rare burger in an old-fashioned diner. Tonino ordered his on a Kaiser roll with red onion, tomato, and lettuce and a dash of Worcestershire sauce.

"This guy's a gent!" remarked one short-order cook.

Wearing a pearl gray suit and a matching Borsalino hat, Tonino must have cut an elegant figure, but he remained a plebeian at heart. When he returned to Rome, he was irked to see swanky nightclubs feature hamburgers as a novelty. Burgers belonged in stands and cafeterias. They symbolized the initiative and enterprise that thrived in America but were impossible in Italy, where a Laocoön of red tape strangled the economy.

For this reason, burgers became a popular lunch item with Rome's business class, from investment bankers to steel magnates, who flaunted their cosmopolitanism and courted the U.S. Ambassador, Clare Boothe Luce. Married to the owner of *Time* and *Fortune,* La Luce was a fierce anti-Communist and the scourge of unions. If Italy did not embrace free-market capitalism, she warned, America would cut foreign aid. Italy got with the program, but paid for its prosperity. Although Luce had coined the term "globaloney" to mock Henry Wallace's internationalism, she paved the way for McDonald's brand of globalization, the ruthless grinding of culture and tradition into paddies. As in Bertold Brecht's "Cannon Song," resistance is futile:

> *And if the population*
> *Should greet us with indignation,*
> *We'll chop 'em to bits,*
> *Because we like our hamburger raw!*

Since 1985, McDonald's has built nearly forty restaurants in Rome, part of its 340 outlets throughout Italy. A McDonald's can be found at Da Vinci Airport and Termini Station, Cinecittà and the Granai Mall, Corso Rinascimento and Palazzo Barberini, the Forum and the Pantheon. Vatican City has not succumbed, but the corporation believes the Pope owes it a favor for having created the Filet-O-Fish sandwich. McDonald's proliferation throughout the Eternal City made Uncle Tonino rabid. He renounced America and died hating Ray Kroc. But the man who brought the Golden Arches to Rome was actually a classics professor named Luigi Salvansechi. As Vice President of Real Estate Development, Salvansechi opened six thousand McDonald's worldwide. Shrewd, perceptive, and self-effacing, he played Marco Polo to Ray Kroc's Kublai Khan.

DR. LUIGI SALVANSECHI immigrated to America in 1959. Thin and solemn, the young professor had earned one PhD in Latin from the University of Rome and another in canon law from the Pontifical Gregorian University. He and his bride had moved to Chicago for the academic job market. Their sponsor, June Martino, was secretary-treasurer of the new McDonald's Corporation. The daughter of a German American druggist, Signora Martino had spent her youth among the Italians on the Windy City's Northwest Side. Clerking in a Neapolitan restaurant, she learned the language, corrected the menu's clumsy English, and illustrated the newspaper ads. Her favorite dish had been *pasta e fagioli,* until Signor Ray Kroc hired her to be his Gal Friday. Overnight, she became a hamburger missionary. A former copywriter, she rebutted a *Fortune* editorial lamenting McDonald's growing defacement of highways. "Uninterrupted scenery can get pretty monotonous," she wrote, claiming the Golden Arches "humanized an overwhelming landscape."

Signora Martino—who was paid in company stock rather than cash and would retire with $70 million—had convinced her husband, a former Motorola technician, to sell his electrical engineering firm and buy a McDonald's stand in Glen Ellyn. Eventually, Lou Martino opened McDonald's research lab in nearby Addison, where he would create a computer that measured the moisture content of cooking fish and cybernetic flyers that assured that French fries achieved a uniform degree of brownness. For now, he offered a grill job to Dottore Salvaneschi, who needed the money. Although his wife had landed an Italian lectureship at Valparaiso University, most area colleges had scrapped Latin. After his second year flipping burgers, Salvaneschi realized he never would teach an Aquinas seminar at Notre Dame, stopped calling himself *professore,* and answered to plain Luigi. Disappointment nearly drove him to drown himself in ketchup.

Hamburgers still repelled him. Since antiquity, Romans rarely eat beef, perhaps because the ancients had venerated the cattle that tilled their fields. Since their toughened flesh made poor meat, oxen were slaughtered only when old, and only during religious festivals. Likewise, the best bulls in the *Forum Boiarum,* the city cattle market, were earmarked for sacrifice to the meat-eating demigod Hercules. The *Ara Maxima,* Rome's great altar, was dedicated to this Olympian and stood in the square the same way the *Charging Bull,* Arturo Di Modica's four-ton bronze statue, stands in Wall Street's Bowling Green Park. Protector of merchants, Hercules symbolized Rome's nouveaux rich: greedy, foul-mouthed, stupid, and mercenary. To honor their muscle-bound patron, toga'ed Rotarians butchered thousands of bullocks at their expense, but the state later subsidized the ritual to celebrate the Republic's GNP.

Apparently, McDonald's had resurrected Rome's classical cult in modern Chicago. The company owned 250 stores and grossed $76 million. Executives must have propitiated the gods of commerce. Luigi pictured a garlanded bull being lead into the boardroom. Sprinkled with corn meal and aspersed with beer, the beast was stunned with a bat and gutted, its liver read for market trends.

A flood of statistics accompanied the torrent of blood. McDonald's sold over 400 million hamburgers, 120 million pounds of French fries, and 400 billion slices of pickle. Within a decade, projections estimated, the company would make twelve billion burgers a year and buy one percent of America's wholesaled beef. Each month ten thousand steers would be fed, slaughtered, processed, frozen in patties, and distributed across a continent. As in a Merrill Lynch spot, the mammoth herd would be large enough to overrun Lower Manhattan. Perhaps the New York Stock Exchange would convert Federal Hall into a *mithraeum* and erect a tauroctony in Signor Kroc's honor. Like the sun god Mithras, guarantor of contracts, he had grabbed by the horns and subdued America's divine bull market.

RAISED IN THE SHADOW of the Union Stockyards, Raymond Albert Kroc would sacrifice more cattle to imperial ambition than all the hecatombs ever offered to Augustus. As Luigi learned from Signora Martino, the *padrone* was born in Oak Park, a mixed neighborhood on Chicago's West Side, on October 5, 1902. Ray's parents considered themselves Americans, even if the German neighbors called them Bohunks. Prosperous relatives ran a restaurant and inn back in the Bohemian village of Plzen, but war and poverty had driven their peasant parents to the New World. Most Oak Park residents were factory hands and stockyard workers, but the Krocs had a toehold in the middle class. Despite a grammar-school education, Louis Kroc had become secretary-treasurer of American District Telegraph, a pokey subsidiary of Western Union. His wife Rose gave occasional piano lessons in their overstuffed parlor.

Forever scouting opportunity, Mr. Kroc bought cheap city lots for potential business use and eventually founded the Pyramid Vacant Real Estate Company. But he lacked the brains and connections to become a successful developer. Even during the boom, the business floundered, and the Krocs' precarious respectability tottered. The Depression finally pushed them over the edge when a stroke felled a weak and besieged Louis Kroc at the office. He left hefty debts and a skimpy life insurance policy. Ironically, as the economy sank, vacant real estate's value soared. Looking back on his father's failure, the *padrone* observed:

"Timing's such a factor in life." An insight worthy of Machiavelli or Dale Carnegie, Luigi thought.

But the *padrone* was destined to succeed. According to family lore, Louis Kroc took his four-year-old son to a phrenologist, who predicted he would make a fortune either in music or food. Rose thought he might become a pianist, since he plunked Dvořák's "Humoresque" in the parlor, but Louis knew the boy was a born salesman. He operated a popcorn and lemonade stand on the front porch, while Papa Kroc peered over the *Chicago Tribune*'s Sunday comics and chuckled. The tiny vendor resembled Danny Dreamer, who could steal a Thanksgiving turkey from a restaurant by stuffing it in his pants and pretending to be Diamond Jim Brady. The lad proved equally incorrigible when he refused to finish school. What was the point? He wanted to be a business-man. What did teachers know about business? That's why McDonald's didn't donate money to higher ed. "Too many bac-calaureates, too few butchers," the *padrone* grunted; which didn't bode well for Luigi. But Signor Kroc always remained grateful to the junior-high debating team for honing his powers of persua-sion. Before dropping out to fight in World War I, he won a dis-trict tournament by proving the health benefits of tobacco.

Fifteen-year-old Ray lied about his age and enlisted in the Red Cross. "I wanted to learn how to operate a car," the future road man joked. As an ambulance driver, he learned loads about meat, plowing through mud with a jostling cargo of mutilated dough-boys. The stockyards back home had provided excellent training for the battlefields of France. Confident and plucky, the skinny teen befriended and inspired his fellow drivers, particularly a fellow Chicagoan from McKinley High named Walt Disney. The same zip served him after the war. Trading *Slavonic Dances* and *Songs My Mother Taught Me* for "Barney Google" and "Yes, We Have No Bananas," he became a barroom pianist. Bouncing on his stool, he played with infectious zest, but the late hours and shady ladies disenchanted him.

Now married, Signor Kroc found stability and direction as a salesman for the Lily-Tulip Paper Cup Company. He could navi-gate Chicago's neighborhoods blindfolded, but immigrant restau-rateurs were immune to his patter. "Naw," they said, "I hev glasses. Dey costs me chipper." More reliable sales could be made in hospital and clinics, but they reeked of disinfectant and reminded him of the war. For extra income, he arranged the music programs and accompanied the singers at WGES.

The Roaring Twenties would cement the *padrone*'s character and beliefs. Like George F. Babbitt, he was a boundless optimist and a cheerful booster. He believed in the gospel of free enterprise and found in the White House a prophet after his own heart. Calvin Coolidge would remain Signor Kroc's lifelong spiritual hero. The president's initials, admirers pointed out, were the same as those of Chamber of Commerce. Shortly after his election, Coolidge summed up the spirit of an entrepreneurial era. "After all," he concluded to a gathering of newspaper editors, "the chief business of the American people is business." A year later he hailed American business as "one of the great contributing forces to the moral and spiritual advancement of the human race." Coolidge provided the creed that bedecked the *padrone*'s office and restaurants—scrolled, framed, and hung on the walls like a plenary indulgence. Luigi knew it by heart:

Press On

Nothing in the World can take the Place of *Persistence*.

**_Talent_ will not.
Nothing is More Common than Unsuccessful Men of Talent.**

**_Genius_ will not.
Unrewarded Genius is Almost a Proverb.**

**_Education_ will not.
The World is full of Educated Derelicts.**

Persistence and Determination alone are Omnipotent!

During the real-estate boom of 1925, the *padrone* tried redeeming his father's dreams. Stuffing his wife and baby daughter in a new Model T, he took the grueling Dixie Highway to Florida. By the time the mud-caked and bug-splattered flivver reached Fort Lauderdale, not one of its original tires was intact. Signor Kroc's sojourn to the Sunshine State proved disastrous. Although salesmanship could make mangrove swamps seem like Eden, prospects always changed their minds upon returning to Connecticut or New Jersey. When impatient Northern bankers stopped lending to pioneering realtors, the bubble burst and left the *padrone* stranded. Forced to tinkle the ivories in a speakeasy called the Silent Night, he yielded to wifely pressure and returned to Chicago and the paper-cup business, bloodied but unbowed.

Unlike his idol Silent Cal, who prudently declined to seek re-election on the eve of the Stock Market Crash, Signor Kroc still believed in capitalism, but the Depression and its aftermath sorely tested his faith. For the next thirty years, he plugged away, a diligent road man ensconced in the middle class but tormented by delusions of grandeur. Now a sales rep for Multimixer, peddling milkshake machines to diners and ice cream parlors, he had grown blocky and compact. He brilliantined his butter-colored hair and wore a bow tie and roomy suits. But the tokens of modest success—his weekly round of bridge, his membership in a second-rate country club, his tidy home in Arlington Heights, one of Chicago's better suburbs—depressed rather than pleased him. At fifty-two, he was past his prime and suffered from diabetes and early arthritis. Years of driving had cost him his gall bladder and most of his thyroid. A cover story in *Forbes* steadily receded to the horizon. "I expected money like you walk into a room and turn on a light switch or a faucet," he confided to Signora Martino. "It wasn't enough."

But his luck changed with an order for eight Multimixers from the McDonald brothers of San Bernardino, California.

"They were a queer pair," the *padrone* later recalled, the kind of provincials out of Nathanael West who come to Hollywood to die. Mac and Dick McDonald had migrated from Bedford, New Hampshire in 1928 to work in movies. For two dour, dutiful Yankees, who looked as if they had been breastfed castor oil, this choice was as inexplicable as their taste for vintage Cadillacs or

the flamboyance of their trademark Golden Arches. But the closest the McDonalds got to the film industry was handling props at
MGM and operating a movie house in Glendora, California,
which they sold in 1940 to open a burger stand in nearby
Pasadena. Eight years later, they created a streamlined self-service
joint in San Bernoo, complete with M-shaped arches. Speedy
service, low prices, and reliable fare made McDonald's Famous
Hamburgers the county's most popular family restaurant. Signor
Kroc, who had traveled two thousand miles to see what kind of
operation needed to make forty-eight milkshakes at once, was
thunderstruck.

"Gentlemen," he said, by way of introduction, "this is the most
efficient money-making machine I have ever seen!" The McDonalds were flattered by Mr. Multimixer, as they called the *padrone*,
until he sprang a proposal: Would the brothers allow him to franchise their business? Mac and Dick were shocked. Good God,
why? They already made $75,000 a year and lived in a big white
house on a hill overlooking the restaurant. Every evening, they sat
on their porch and relished the desert sunset. A new venture
would create only problems. A skillful debater, the *padrone* parried
this objection. Franchising, he argued, would *ensure* the brothers'
quiet life. Signor Kroc would sow the franchise licenses while the
McDonalds reaped the royalty checks. "I'll take the headaches,
you keep the sunsets," he said.

Behind their grill, the brothers wavered. The *padrone* felt as if
he had dragged his tie in a bowl of pea soup. Finally, Mac gave a
little wince that passes for a smile in New England. The brothers
agreed but drove a hard bargain. Signor Kroc had asked for 2 percent of all the gross sales of any franchised store but settled for 1.9
percent, out of which he also had to pay the McDonalds 5 percent. His actual take, therefore, was only 1.4 percent. Nevertheless, he now possessed the coveted McDonald's name and with
that crowbar brought down the brothers. Claiming his contract's
proprietary stipulations had left him vulnerable, he offered to buy
out his partners. The brothers asked for $2.7 million. When
Signor Kroc heard the price in his downtown Chicago office, he
dropped the phone. "What was that?" Dick asked on the other
end of the line. Signor Kroc replied, "Me jumping off the twentieth floor of the LaSalle-Wacker Building!"

A battery of college endowment funds agreed to a five-year loan at an exorbitant annual interest, so the $2.7 million ultimately cost $14 million. But after securing the trademarks, copyrights, formulas, and arches, the *padrone* obliterated the McDonalds. Within months, two Golden Arches loomed across the road from the brothers' beloved restaurant, renamed Mac's Place. Spotless, red-and-white tiled, the stand replicated theirs, except it was called McDonald's. Unable to compete with the allure of their forfeited name, the brothers sold their house and business and returned to New Hampshire. No more desert sunsets for them.

Like a true prince, the *padrone* never apologized for his cruelty. "Look," he explained in a magazine interview, "it's ridiculous to call this an industry. This is not. This is rat eat rat, dog eat dog. I'll kill 'em, and I'm gonna kill 'em before they kill me. You're talking about the American way of survival of the fittest."

Vengeance is a dish best served deep-fried.

SIGNOR KROC EXPANDED and Taylorized the McDonald brothers' system. He required all restaurants to serve a hamburger in fifty seconds. To achieve such uniformity, production became a precise science. A basic machine-cut patty must weigh 1.6 ounces, measure 3.875 inches in diameter, and contain no lungs, hearts, cereal, or soybeans. Each pound of meat should equal ten hamburgers, each containing no more than nineteen percent fat. Everything was calculated, from the exact size of the bun (three-and-a-half inches wide) to the amount of onions (one quarter ounce). For the fastest browning, the bun needed the highest sugar content. Freshness mattered more than thrift. French fries were to be discarded after seven minutes, hamburgers after ten, coffee after thirty.

This patty-to-patron assembly line was supported by a network of suppliers, truckers, and outlets and serviced by a cadre of managers, assistants, crew members, field inspectors, and district supervisors, whose *esprit de corps* came from strict rules and colorful arcana. Educated at the Vatican, Luigi admired this strategy. After all, the Church had conquered the world and united the faithful through the monogram IHS ("*Iesus Hominum Salvator*"). McDonald's had condensed its corporate theology into six letters:

QSC/TLC ("Quality, Service, and Cleanliness with Tender Loving Care").

"I believe in God, family, and McDonald's," Signor Kroc declared. "And in the office that order is reversed." The company cultivated a wholesome image. Norman Rockwell was commissioned to paint "The Happy Adventure," which showed idealized children crowding a McDonald's counter. But the smiles and freckles hid a Jesuitical zeal. The *padrone* wanted America to have as many white shirts and crew hats as China had Mao jackets and little red books. After converting middling cities such as Perth Amboy, Terre Haute, and Tucson, he missionized suburbia. Leasing a plane, he crisscrossed the country and scouted territory with binoculars.

Through cracks in the clouds, he noted traffic intersections, subdivisions, shopping centers, industrial parks. From the air, he targeted the fussy, the clean, and the proud. Churchgoers qualified, so he counted steeples. McDonald's, he believed, would save these God-fearing folks from rock 'n roll, juvenile delinquents, fellow travelers, and agitators. By equating the good of the company with the good of the country, he destroyed all rivals with a clean conscience. "If my competitor were drowning," he admitted, "I'd stick a hose in his mouth and turn on the water." Such a man expected single-minded dedication in a subordinate.

Luigi Salvanseschi worked his way up from janitor to assistant manager of the Glenn Ellyn McDonald's. When Lou Martino left to head R&D, the *professore* became the boss and created what may have been the company's first formal operations lesson. Dissatisfied with how the crew was greeting customers, he wrote what he called a "Windowman Lesson," sat his staff on shortening cans in the basement, and lectured on Castaglione. Just because they lived in a democracy, he said, didn't mean they shouldn't treat their customers like royalty. He assigned homework and awarded bonuses when they improved. Except for the Chicago flagship, his stand became the busiest and most profitable in the state. Between rushes, he unwound with Horace.

Luigi's elegant memos and reports, seasoned with historical references and literary quotations, caught Ray Kroc's perplexed attention. June Martino suggested he interview the *professore* for a corporate position. The chairman was amused. Despite the accent, the little guy's vocabulary was bigger than his, and he read classical Latin for relaxation. He mentioned Oscar Mayer and Guicciardini in the same sentence, claimed McDonald's symbolized "a society on wheels," recounted how Buffalo Bill had tried to recruit the *butteri*, the cowboys of the Tuscan Maremma, into his Wild West show, and proposed the company redesign its red-and-white tile buildings. Was this wop nuts?

Whatever his faults, Ray Kroc recognized and nurtured talent, no matter how eccentric. As an audition, Luigi was sent to Manhattan Beach, California, to manage a McOpCo, the first company-operated restaurant, and to explore future sites. Since Americans were lazy, these stands had to be placed where patrons would smack against the glass. Salvansechi proved such a talented location scout that Kroc promoted him to Vice President of Real Estate Administration. The boys back in Oak Grove rolled their eyes, but they didn't know Luigi like Ray knew Luigi. Familiar with city planning and engineering, the Roman *professore* made all roads lead to the Golden Arches. He also possessed the will and confidence to take on the *padrone* if he believed he was right.

"Signor Kroc," he chided, "California is setting the national trend for community planning. How can we go into these towns and propose to put up these slat-roofed eyesores?" The chairman fumed, but Luigi carried on about Vitruvius and Michelangelo until he prevailed. McDonald's replaced its Jetsons-style, candy-striped drive-thru with a more family-friendly building, complete with mansard roof, pressed brick exterior, and indoor seating.

Over the next twenty years, Salvaneschi contributed to McDonald's growth in two ways. First, he persuaded the company to open restaurants in small communities off the beaten path. This idea developed from a theory the *professore* called the Monotony Index. Simply put, the higher the level of monotony in a town, the better McDonald's chances of doing business there. In big cities chock-full of shops and restaurants, McDonald's was only one of thousands of choices. But in areas with nothing to do on Sunday afternoons, McDonald's would be instantly popular. The Rust Belt was full of dead-end places with a high monotony index. Forgotten by industry and bypassed by superhighways and shopping malls, these people would become grateful and loyal McDonald's patrons. As the Romans knew, the heart of the Republic is in

the boonies. The *padrone* was skeptical, but Luigi's patriotic senti-
ment proved bankable. Even isolated franchises in Nebraska and
Wyoming averaged eighty thousand dollars a month.

Second, Salvanseschi encouraged McDonald's to become
international. Before the 1970s, foreign expansion had been ham-
pered by Chairman Kroc's limitations. European and Asian
investors disliked ostentation, and Kroc owned a $4.5 million jet
and a Palladian mansion with a doorbell that chimed "You
Deserve a Break Today!" True, he cut a commanding figure—the
thin hair brushed straight back, the custom-made blazers impec-
cably crisp, the gimlet eyes forever checking surfaces for cleanliness and order—but his manners were boorish. The bulky rings
on his fingers glinted as he gobbled a hamburger with both
hands. Stubbornly provincial, Kroc resisted a makeover, until
Luigi convinced him of McDonald's mission. As the United States
floundered in the quagmire of Vietnam, the hamburger needed
to triumph abroad. This proposal appealed to the *padrone*, whose
reactionary politics were no secret.

Like his pal Walt Disney, Ray Kroc was a fanatical Cold War-
rior. To emulate the space race, he had hired a NASA engineer to
make Hamburger Central, McDonald's headquarters, a cross
between Kafka's insurance office and Kubrick's *2001*. The sev-
enth-floor think tank, a hermetically sealed capsule, included a
biofeedback machine and a silk-screen burger floating in the
Milky Way. As a rebuke to Columbia and Berkley, Kroc founded
Hamburger University, a training center where students received
bachelor's and master's degrees in Hamburgerology and were
indoctrinated in company ideology.

"We've found we can't trust nonconformists," Kroc lectured.
"We make conformists out of them. The organization can't trust
the individual; the individual must trust the organization."

When Watts exploded, Kroc invited right-wing commentator
Paul Harvey to lecture black franchisees on the futility of violence
and the dangers of welfare. A former Goldwater supporter, Kroc
was a favorite at Republican fundraisers. His high-school forensics
background made him a strong orator. "The only way we can
advance is by going forward," he declared, "individually and col-
lectively, in the spirit of the pioneer. We must take the risks

involved in our free enterprise system. That is the only way in the world to economic freedom. There is no other way."

Only Richard Nixon, Kroc believed, could save capitalism from regulators and subversives. Besides being a veteran Red-baiter, Nixon had been a hamburger lover since early youth. In his first presidential bid, he contrasted his fast-food tastes with the presumably fancier fare enjoyed by his millionaire opponent John F. Kennedy. Whistle-stopping though the Midwest, Nixon tearfully recalled how Depression-era customers bought hamburger rather than steak from his parents' Whittier grocery store. ("Stew meat rather than chuck roast," Nixon clarified. "Chuck roast was too expensive.") By the next stop, the candidate claimed to have ground the meat himself. Ironically, a burger scandal may have cost Nixon the close election. An investigative reporter revealed how the former Veep had finessed a $205,000 loan from Howard Hughes so his brother Donald could save the family restaurant, which featured the Nixonburger. The diner still failed and the loan was never repaid, but Ray thought the effort did Nixon credit. Eight years later, he helped place Nixon in the Oval Office.

McDonald's became the new administration's favorite cash cow. Nixon and Kroc formed a mutual admiration society. The president called the burger king "an American success story," and the burger king called the president "the protector of free enter-prise." In 1972, McDonald's donated some $250,000 to the Com-mittee to Re-Elect the President (CREEP). In exchange, the White House promised price-control exemption on the Big Mac, a fast-food monopoly at all public events for the upcoming bicen-tennial, and a congressional bill reducing the minimum wage for American teens by twenty percent.

After the election, Kroc was invited to a banquet in the State Dining Room. The black-tie affair was reserved for the cream of American capitalism, including Henry Ford II, construction tycoon Del Webb, and computer millionaire and future presiden-tial candidate Ross Perot, whom Kroc had met when they both received the Horatio Alger Award. The magnates and tycoons assembled to shake hands with the president, who seemed a bit shy. When Nixon came to Ray Kroc, he extended his hand and wiggled a finger.

"What is it now," Nixon asked, "eight or nine billion?"

"Mr. President," Kroc said portentously, "it's twelve billion."

The finger stopped wiggling, and the two men grasped hands. "My goodness," Nixon said with hushed awe, "isn't that wonderful?"

If Nixon could go to China, Luigi joked, Kroc could go to France. But to compete in a global market, shuttle diplomacy must replace Chicago street fighting. To quote a proverb: "*Paese che vai, usanze che trove.*" When in Rome, do as the Romans do. Like ambassadors, company reps must familiarize themselves with a country's language, history, and customs. Balance sheets alone won't work.

AS MCDONALD'S MINISTER Plenipotentiary, Dottore Salvaneschi brought the Golden Arches to eighty-six different countries. Some markets were chosen for propaganda purposes. When Volkswagen and Honda encroached on the U.S. auto market, and Pizza Hut and Little Caesar challenged the hamburger's fast-food hegemony, McDonald's targeted the former Axis Powers. Germany proved a soft touch. A special envoy presented a Big Mac to the Mayor of Hamburg, who grinned and said, "*Ich bin ein Hamburger!*"

Japan surrendered before war was declared. Increasingly Westernized, the country faced mass consumer unrest. Housewives demonstrated against the high cost of living; newspapers bristled with reports of environmental damage and pollution. The traditional Japanese diet, charged nutritionists, doctors, and consumer advocates, had become toxic. Fish and rice were contaminated. Farms suffered from mercury and cadmium poisoning. So when McDonald's premiered in the Ginza, Tokyo's commercial and entertainment center, families flocked. Because the Golden Arches resembled a Shinto temple, restaurants spread throughout the archipelago. When a McDonald's opened in downtown Hiroshima, near where the first atomic bomb had exploded, Japanese businessmen cheered. "If we eat hamburgers for a thousand years," one declared, "we will become blond. And when we become blond, we will conquer the world."

Italy, however, proved intractable. Initial surveys and focus groups were discouraging. "This shit isn't fit for cats," said one Roman teen. McDonald's faced competition from two hundred and fifty thousand family restaurants. Autogrill, Italy's leading roadside cafeteria chain, virtually monopolized the national highway system. Even so, an overt challenge would have been suicide. Italians expect their corporations to function like cooperatives, so McDonald's was obliged to court powerful suppliers. These *fornitori* demanded and got prominent billing on all company materials. Their logos were displayed like the district flags at the Palio di Siena: INALCA provided the beef for McDonald's Italia's *panini*, Gruppo Amadori the chicken for its *bocconcini di polo*, Italpatate the spuds for its *patate fritte*, Eisberg Italia the greens for its *insalate*. This was Renaissance capitalism, the *professore* explained. Vestiges of the old client-patron system still operated within the free market. If McDonald's was to catch on, its management and franchisees must be completely Italian as soon as possible. Cronyism should be tolerated, even encouraged.

Despite sound advice and careful planning, progress stalled. Over the next decade, fewer than forty McDonald's opened in Italy. In contrast, France boasted nearly a thousand, despite the scandal surrounding the Big Mac. The sandwich's French name, *Gros Mec*, was slang for pimp. McDonald's bootstrapped further growth by acquiring Burghy, Italy's only hamburger chain, but the eighty units mattered less than the government contacts. At least bureaucrats could be bribed. Intellectuals were implacable. After McDonald's came to Rome's Piazza di Spagna, journalist Carlo Petrini founded the Slow Food Movement. Adopting the snail as its mascot, the group published a manifesto denouncing American fast food. The public relations office was perplexed. It could handle a Basque farmer's driving a tractor into a restaurant. How could it respond to crusaders who called themselves "eco-gastronomists" and lobbied for the purple asparagus of Albenga, the black celery of Trevi, the Vesuvian apricot, the Paduan hen, long-tailed sheep from Laticauda, succulent Sienese pigs once popular in the courts of medieval Tuscany, and a host of endangered handmade cheeses and salamis known to a dozen old peasants?

When Dottore Salvansechi left to head Blockbuster Video, McDonald's Italia was rocked by a series of crises. At a franchise in Florence's *centro storico*, the unionized crew protested intimidating work conditions. The revolt spread to Rome, where a manager's browbeating a cashier sparked a wildcat strike at a McDonald's on the capital's main ring road. No sooner had these labor problems subsided, when *vacca matta* (mad cow disease) was discovered in a Modena slaughterhouse. Government health ministers ordered the public to avoid McDonald's. Resentful over lost profits and growing media criticism, the chain sued restaurant critic Edoardo Raspelli for claiming its food "oppressed the human palate." This litigation proved as effective as Oscar Wilde's libel suit against the Marquess of Queensbury. The company's defense of its culinary standards and its request for $25 million in damages was laughed out of court. National sympathy was aroused after a jihadist exploded a car bomb in the Brescia drive-thru, but everyone cheered the Apulian baker who drove the local McDonald's out of business.

LOCATED TWENTY-FIVE MILES south of Bari, Altamura has been known for its golden, coarse-grained bread since the fifth century B.C. Originally called Altilia, from *Alter Ilium* (the "other Troy"), the town was founded by Antellus, a friend of Aeneas, whose burial mound is nearby. But the town cares more about bread than myths. The ancient recipe requires durum whole-wheat flour with yeast, water, and sea salt. Baked in open oak wood ovens and preserved with fragrant herbs, this bread was meant for shepherds and farmers who worked far from home.

Because it remains fresh for days or even weeks at a time, Horace, who stopped in Altilia on his way to Brundisium, called it "by far the best bread to be had, so good that the wise traveler takes a supply of it for his onward journey." For historical reasons, then, Altamura's bread was the first and only to be granted a DOP certificate. DOP stands for Denominazione d'Origine Protetta (Denomination of Protected Origin). Since DOP products must be specific to a geographic area, the region's flour, which resembles gold dust, is ground in mills within the communes of Altamura, Gravina di Puglia, Poggiorsini, Spinazzola, and Minervino Murge.

Altamura's sixty-five thousand residents are proud to live in the City of Bread. Nevertheless, they were surprised when McDonald's sought permission to open a restaurant in the main square, Piazza Zanardelli. The mayor and city council agreed. The twenty-five new jobs were welcome, and what was wrong with a little

Americanization? The old timers fondly recalled the GIs who had liberated them from the Fascists. They were not prepared for another occupation. Violating construction permits, McDonald's mounted its huge arches on a steel pole near the *municipio*. The yellow neon glared off the rose window of Altamura's thirteenth-century cathedral and disturbed the falcons nesting in the trees. When McDonald's refused to comply with town ordinances, war was declared. Peppino Colamonico, a doctor, and Onofrio Pepe, a retired journalist, formed a grassroots group called the Friends of Cardoncello, named after Apulia's celebrated mushroom. Civilized and pacific, these culinary partisans foreswore all violence and coercion. McDonald's had issued a challenge, but it was not a challenge to confront in rage. Friendly competition was better. If the Americans had their fast food, the Altamurani had theirs.

Luca DiGesù, a fourth-generation baker, opened a small shop right next to McDonald's. Specializing in flat breads, Antica Casa DiGesù barely siphoned customers attracted to the spot's novelty. The McDonald's manager found the local color quaint, until Luca began baking *panini,* bread rolls stuffed with various fillings, single or combined: *mortadella, mozzarella, scamorza,* eggs, basil, and tomato. Gradually, he included seasonal fare. In spring, he made *fèdda,* a local version of *bruschetta*—toasted bread drizzled with olive oil and salt and smothered in chopped tomatoes. In winter, he served *cialda,* a hearty bread soup. Luca lined a pot with sliced *focaccia* then added water, onions, tomatoes, parsley, basil, potatoes, olive oil, olives, celery, and lemons. By now, he had an audience. Locals were deserting the McDonald's in droves, and the bakery was attracting out-of-towners from as far away as Bari. Not a lira had been spent on advertising. Word of mouth was enough. It was simple economics. For the same price as a processed burger, people could buy a hunk of heavenly *focaccia.*

McDonald's was stunned. How could this Jedi baker win without a marketing strategy, without promotions, discounts, tie-ins, and giveaways? Panicked, the empire struck back. It offered school trips to visit its kitchens, free restaurant access for birthday parties, coupons for the *bambini.* Ronald McDonald gave English lessons. As a last resort, a TV was installed so the townies could watch soccer, but after a game, customers would go next-door for some *focaccia.* The fact that the landlord was Luca's brother-in-law probably didn't help. After two years, the McDonald's went broke and disappeared overnight. The long red carpet was rolled up and secreted away. The Golden Arches were dismantled and surreptitiously packed. The windows were shrouded like the dead on a battlefield. Not a trace remains. Today a jeans store and a bank share the former restaurant site. According to Patrick Girdoni, a Chicago entrepreneur who had returned to live in his ancestral home, the victory belonged to Altamura as well as Luca DiGesù. "McDonald's didn't get beat by a baker," he said. "McDonald's got beat by a culture."

UNCLE TONINO TOLD ME the news. He was pleased to see McDonald's routed but doubted it would stop its takeover of Italy. "In no way is this a defeat," contended Mario Resca, president of McDonald's Italia. "If anything, I'm proud the local culture appreciates its regional cuisine. It means McDonald's has stimulated a healthy competition, and can reciprocate in kind."

Resca vowed to double Italy's number of franchises in five years. Once Hamburger Central committed resources, Tonino said, it would be total war. To paraphrase Stalin, how many divisions does Carlo Petrini command? The Slow Food Foundation boasts eighty-two thousand members, but these academics, gourmets, and food critics are scattered all over the world and lack the political and financial clout to take on McDonald's. "It will be the Polish Calvary against the Panzers," Tonino said. McDonald's owns thirty thousand restaurants in a hundred and twenty countries and employs over a million workers. It trains more people than the U.S. Army and operates more bases than NATO. It conquers and reconstructs enemy nations. The world's busiest McDonald's stands in Moscow's Pushkin Square and serves forty thousand people every day. The world's largest McDonald's occupies Tiananmen Square and seats eight hundred patrons. Like the Borg, it absorbs all cultures. Israeli McDonald's feature kosher burgers while Indian McDonald's offer the Maharaja Mac, a poultry version of the Big Mac, and the McAloo Tikki, a vegetarian version. For these and other reasons, the *Economist* uses a Big Mac Index to measure the purchasing power of foreign currencies. McDonald's hold on the global economy made it unstoppable. One might as well imagine stopping the next Ice Age.

Tonino's pessimism puzzled me. True, McDonald's bestrode the world like a colossus, but hadn't its fast-food empire been hamstrung in Italy? Tonino sighed and explained a paradox. McDonald's was stopped by the same forces that have prevented Italy from achieving social and economic stability for the past century: aggressive trade unions, sclerotic bureaucracy, feisty provincialism, and shameless nepotism. Such dysfunction protects tradition from the ruthless efficiency of globalization, but can Italy still afford to do so? Saddled with the West's lowest birthrate and addicted to social programs, Italy is becoming a stagnant gerontocracy. Unless the government wants to instigate a massive brain drain, economic policy must change, and that means coming to terms with such companies as McDonald's.

Like Milan's disintegrating cathedral or Venice's endangered wetlands, regional cuisines cost much to preserve. Italy's thwarted but influential professional class may consider the project too expensive. American pop culture and consumerism have whetted the appetite of youth, even in remote Abruzzo. Frustrated teens from my father's mountain village joyride to the Vasto McDonald's for a hamburger spree. Defying schoolteacher, priest, and police sergeant, they deliberately litter the Piazza Municipio with grease-stained wrappers and napkins.

"It's a question of choice," said Luca DiGesù, after driving McDonald's from Altamura. But how free are we to choose in the New World Order? Tonino asked me this question shortly before he died, and it still stumps me. But I suspect the answer depends on the trajectory of late capitalism. If globalization truly liberates and empowers all countries, as proponents claim, the world might feast on a smorgasbord of democracy—provided we recognize prosperity's limits. "A firm defense of quiet material pleasure," states the Slow Food Manifesto, "is the only way to oppose the universal folly of Fast Life."

Striking a balance between decadence and asceticism, these words are worthy of Horace, the Epicurean who treasured the simple taste of cheese and olives. An auctioneer's son, the poet offered the following prayer to his patron Mercury, the god of commerce and gab, who had blessed him with a Sabine farm: "If I do nothing crooked to make this place bigger; if I do nothing stupid to make it smaller; if I neither uproot stakes to move my property line nor dig like a gopher for buried treasure; in short, if I'm happy with what I have; then fatten my livestock, fatten my bank book, fatten everything except my head!"

However, if globalization merely serves corporate feudalism and cultural hegemony, the backlash could be terrible. Are Colombian bean pickers less exploited because McDonald's serves Lavazza Coffee? Is the environment less damaged because Tuscan and Texas ranchers have created a hybrid steer called the Chiangus? Without wisdom and compassion, the world will degenerate into a Thyestean banquet. Capitalism will cannibalize the planet and choke on its own gore. If that occurs, we will not snack with Horace but lunch with Trimalchio.

At the end of the *Satyricon*, the parasites who have filched scraps from the millionaire's table arrive at Crotone, where the hustler Eumolpus dictates his will. With the exception of his freedmen, he stipulates, all heirs must slice his body into pieces and swallow them before witnesses. Those who do not comply will be disinherited, but Eumolpus is sure greed will overcome repugnance. What is the nausea of an hour compared to the boon of a lifetime? Close your eyes, he instructs, and imagine that, instead of human flesh, you're munching a million. If that's not enough, lawyers will concoct some gravy to kill the taste. "After all," he offers, "no meat is truly savory until it has been seasoned and marinated."

Makes you wonder about the Big Mac's special sauce. Crotone, in fact, a cultural center of Magna Graecia and a battleground in the Second Punic War, is slated to become the home of Calabria's sixth McDonald's. What else can I do but savor the irony? After all, it was an Italian American franchisee, Jim Delligatti, who invented the Big Mac in 1967. To celebrate its fortieth anniversary, eighty-nine-year-old Delligatti opened the Big Mac Museum Restaurant near Pittsburgh, featuring a fourteen-foot-high and twelve-foot-wide statue of the world's favorite sandwich.

Billions and billions served, *paisan*—and I'm lovin' it!

ENVOY

Nightcap

Top of the World

NIGHTCAP

WHENEVER RUMORS of another terrorist attack make sleep impossible, I turn to my liquor cabinet, a more reliable defense than the Department of Homeland Security. Despite human wickedness, civilization can distill truth and comfort in pleasurable ways. Sometimes I take a nip of Vecchia Romagna brandy or a snort of Bortolo Nardini grappa but since boyhood, my favorite drink has been Averna Amaro.

Because of its dark color and narcotic effect, some people think this powerful cordial is named after Lago d'Averno, a volcanic crater lake west of Naples. Called Avernus in classical times, it was considered the gateway to the Underworld. Actually, the drink is named after Salvatore Averna, a textile manufacturer from Caltanissetta, Sicily, who in 1868 adapted the recipe from a local Benedictine abbey. A medicinal blend of herbs, roots, citrus rinds, and caramel, Averna now graces every Italian home. Its luscious texture, concentrated palate, and exquisite bitterness make it a perfect *digestivo* (digestive) or *bicchierino primo di andare a letto* (nightcap). I take mine neat, whatever the occasion or weather.

Such unimaginative provincialism always irked Uncle Tonino. "His father herded goats until he left for America," he once jibed. "Let him lap from a trough!" A born sophisticate, Tonino preferred two classic Averna cocktails: La Dolce Vita and La Dura Vita, respectively, Easy Street and Hard Times. Which one he drank depended on how well the stock market had performed that day. Supposedly, these complementary recipes come from the legendary Count Camillo Negroni, an early twentieth-century nobleman and *bon vivant*, who spent his youth dallying in an American rodeo before returning to Florence and becoming a permanent fixture at the Giacosa bar on Via Tornabuoni.

LA DOLCE VITA

INGREDIENTS
- 2 ounces Campari
- 1 ounce Averna Amaro
- 2 to 3 ounces club soda or mineral water
- 1 lemon twist

INSTRUCTIONS
1. Fill a collins glass with ice.
2. Pour liquids, stir, and garnish with twist.
3. Sip and smile.

LA DURA VITA

INGREDIENTS
- 1 ½ ounces gin
- 1 ounce Campari
- ½ ounce Averno Amaro
- 1 lemon twist

INSTRUCTIONS
1. Fill an old-fashioned glass with ice.
2. Pour liquids, stir, and garnish with twist.
3. Sip and frown.

But even Count Negroni would have balked at the elaborate Averna cocktails served at the Greatest Bar on Earth, once the World Trade Center's fashionable watering hole in the sky, now a Valhalla to America's lost prosperity, where dead celebrities forever swap portfolio tips and dead bartenders still insist on being called "mixologists." During the heady boom years, Papa sometimes took me to here for a nightcap, if a business dinner kept us late in the city. The floor-to-ceiling windows made the panoramic view more intoxicating than the booze.

One evening, an aggressively cheerful young bartender—who claimed to have been Tom Cruise's understudy in *Cocktail*—tried to impress us. With great flourish, he combined a bottle of ginger ale, a half ounce of lemon juice, and two ounces of Averna in a highball glass and served the sparkling elixir to my father with a lime wedge and a smirk.

Papa looked at the drink skeptically. "This concoction have a name?" he asked.

"Vertigo," the bartender replied.

"What else," I said.

TOP OF THE WORLD

SEPTEMBER 11 wiped out my Rolodex. Many former classmates, colleagues, and clients perished in the attacks. My sister, a vice president at J.P. Morgan, was spared because she had cancelled a presentation to take her infant son to the doctor. But Windows on the World, the elegant penthouse restaurant in the North Tower of the World Trade Center, was destroyed. During the Reagan era, my parents used Windows on the World as a deprogramming room. Whenever I read too much Dorothy Day, criticized Milton Friedman, or thought of chucking advertising to pursue a PhD or to write the next *Grapes of Wrath*, they would wine and dine me at Windows on the World. They wanted me to know what I would lose if I stepped off the velvet treadmill.

Designed by Joe Baum, who had created such landmarks as the Four Seasons, La Fonda del Sol, and the aptly named Forum of the Twelve Caesars, the restaurant spanned an entire acre, fifty thousand square feet of velvet, tile, and glass, and specialized in New American cuisine. Three words, three lies. Only an idiot, I groused at our first luncheon, would trade a simple bowl of *pasta e fagioli* for this pretentious wild mushroom bisque. As for the Caesar salad, the Romaine had been printed at the Federal Mint but the croutons were soaked in oil. If a yuppie had devoured a *zeppola* at the San Gennaro festival and then wiped his mouth with a paisley tie, I could not have been more appalled. Supposedly, James Beard and Jacques Pépin had developed the menu, but it tasted like airport food, designed for a frequent-flyer class whose world fits into a briefcase.

The food was irrelevant, Papa explained. People came here to eat the money.

With annual revenues of $37 million, Windows on the World was America's highest-grossing restaurant, so its cachet surpassed the Sky Club's or the Rainbow Room's. For this reason, claustrophobic publicists endured a five-minute elevator ride, unkempt bohemians submitted to a corporate dress code, and snooty wine critics paid three thousand dollars for a dubious bottle of 1928 Chateau Lafite-Rothschild. A six-month wait for a reservation was routine, but Papa's Seventh-Avenue clout always secured a table.

I preferred Angelo's on Mulberry Street but still admired the panoramic view: New Jersey, the Hudson, Midtown, Uptown, the Bronx, the East River, Brooklyn, and Queens. From 107 stories up, the horizon actually curved. On bright days, the skyline shimmered and eastern Long Island was a polished emerald. On gray days, snow fell up and clouds tutued the Empire State Building. Below Olympus, the Wall Street traffic was a Matchbox set, and traffic choppers hovered like dragonflies over Roosevelt Drive.

ALL THIS COULD BE MINE, Papa preached, if I wised up and stopped knocking America. Didn't I know this was the greatest country in the world? Where else could a shepherd boy from Abruzzo, who had never owned a dress shirt until his Confirmation, create haute couture for politicians and starlets? The wait staff nodded and beamed. Coming from Angola, Bangladesh, Columbia, Egypt, Guyana, Jamaica, and Thailand, they believed in the American Gospel. Their faith, hope, and charity sustained them and made tolerable the boorishness of their so-called betters.

Often, I wanted to hurl the beautiful people off the South Tower observation deck. Junior brokers from Cantor Fitzgerald jockey to break in American Express cards. A shapely Republican fundraiser smokes a Montecristo and explains how Ayn Rand can change her Mexican busboy's life. Norman Mailer threatens the wine steward with an ice bucket. Mick Jagger orders a waiter to snatch a camera away from Andy Warhol, who insists on snapping pictures. A drunken investor baits the Ugandan ambassador: "What did the cannibal say when he threw up the missionary? You can't keep a good man down!"

When I glower, Papa chides me. If the staff were being such good sports, why couldn't I? Yes, these people were swine, but swine dig up truffles. You don't need good people to have a good society, thank God, only good things. Ignore the jerks. Instead, admire America's beauty and power.

Che meraviglia! What a wonder!

TEN YEARS LATER, Italian newlyweds uttered these very words when they entered Windows on the World. Arriving at 9:00 P.M. on Monday, September 10, 2001, they were seated at table 64, the last in the dining room. Thrilled by the view, the starry-eyed bride asked about the bridges and buildings. The groom, who ran a cheese factory in Parma, showed his business card to the steward, Carlos Medina.

At 11:30, the couple asked for the check. The captain presented the bill, but when Carlos retired to the kitchen to process the credit card, the company denied payment—a common problem with foreign cards. Very politely, in Italian, Carlos informed the groom, who asked if the 107th floor had an ATM. The only machine was down in the lobby, but Carlos escorted the guest in the elevator. When the pair returned, it was past midnight. After paying the tab, the newlyweds had little left for a tip, so the groom gave Carlos twenty dollars plus a hundred thousand liras. Suddenly, the couple realized they had no money to return to their hotel. Carlos chivalrously returned the twenty for cab fare and accepted another fifty thousand liras.

The grateful newlyweds would be among the restaurant's six surviving guests.

ON THE MORNING OF September 11, Windows on the World served breakfast on two levels. Wild Blue, the restaurant's intimate aerie, entertained the movers and shakers who worked and played in the World Trade Center. Early risers with deluxe day planners, this small but select group, less than a dozen, usually arrived at 7:30 A.M. and chatted with manager Doris Eng. The downstairs ballroom was reserved for the Waters Financial Technology Congress. Risk Waters Group Ltd., a London firm providing risk management, market data, and computational finance, had arranged a splendid buffet of fresh fruit, Irish oatmeal, scrambled eggs, and sliced smoked salmon for its sixteen representatives and seventy-one conference participants.

"I was sitting facing the Statue of Liberty," recalls Liz Thompson, executive director of the Lower Manhattan Cultural Council and a Wild Blue regular. "And it was a gorgeous, gorgeous morning. We all commented on what a perfect day it was."

Perhaps it was the company. Thompson breakfasted with Geoffrey Wharton, an executive with Silverstein Properties, which had just leased the Twin Towers. At the next table sat Michael Nestor, the deputy inspector general of the Port Authority of New York and New Jersey, and one of his investigators, Richard Tierney. Both worked on the thirty-first floor of the North Tower. Nearby, alone at a window table and reading the *New York Times*, was their boss Neil D. Levin. The new executive director of the Port Authority, who had never eaten before at Wild Blue, seemed to be waiting for someone. He nodded abstractly. At a fourth table kibitzed six prominent stockbrokers, including Emeric "Ric" Harvey, the energetic president of Harvey Young Yurman Inc.

The cobalt blue September sky filled every window, and Doris Eng's radiant smile matched the weather. A New York University graduate, who still shared an apartment in Flushing, Queens with her immigrant mother, Eng had worked at Le Cirque, the Mayfield, and the Warwick, before landing her dream job at Windows on the World. Today she had a special treat for Ric Harvey, two prized tickets to *The Producers*, compliments of her fellow manager Jules Roinnel. It was the perfect gift. Like Max Bialystock, Harvey was a larger-than-life go-getter with a bullhorn voice. As a teen, he had sold truck rides to children with his friend Ray in Sheepshead Bay, Brooklyn. "Come swing and sway with Ric and Ray!" he would bellow. Eventually, his brash voice roared above the din of the American Stock Exchange.

"Flaunt it, baby! Flaunt it!"

Harvey's Zero Mostel impression won a faint smile from waiter Jan Maciejewski. With brown-green eyes and a springy build, he cut an elegant figure even as he darted around the room, refilling coffee cups and taking orders. An avid soccer and tennis player, the thirty-nine-year-old Polish immigrant was always running. He would dash from his main job at Windows on the World to catch the subway to his other job as a computer consultant. Then he would dash back to the subway to get home to his wife in Astoria, Queens. His pockets were often stuffed with Band-Aids for his blistered feet. This morning he was filling in for a colleague at Wild Blue's breakfast shift.

Every hand was needed. Most of the Windows staff was at the downstairs conference. Eighty-seven famished guests had arrived, including top executives from Merrill Lynch and UBS Warburg. Some exhibitors already tended their booths, set up in the Horizon Suite across the hallway. A picture taken that morning shows two exhibitors, Peter Alderman and William Kelly, salesmen for Bloomberg L.P., chatting with a colleague beside a table filled with a multi-screened computer display. Stuart Lee and Garth Feeney, two vice presidents of Data Synapse, ran displays of their new software. Latecomers were urged to raid the buffet before the conference's nine o'clock keynote. The omelet bar was to die for.

Upstairs, Neil Levin read his newspaper. Mike Nestor and Dick Tierney were a little curious to see whom the boss was meeting for breakfast. But it was getting late. Nestor had a meeting at the International Trade Centre on the seventy-eighth floor, so he and Tierney headed for the elevators, stopping at Levin's table to say goodbye. Behind them rushed Liz Thompson and Geoff Wharton. Nestor held the door, and the two hopped in. Then the doors closed, and the elevator began its descent.

It was 8:44 A.M.

TWO MINUTES LATER, an explosion ten floors below rocked Windows on the World. American Flight 11 had crashed into the North Tower. Measuring 156 feet from wing tip to wing tip, the Boeing 767 had hit the North Tower at four-hundred-seventy miles an hour. The jet tore through the offices of Marsh & McLennan Companies, shredding steel columns, wallboard, filing cabinets, and computer desks. Ten thousand gallons of fuel ignited and incinerated everything. The landing gear hurtled through the south side of the building and wound up five blocks away on Rector Street.

The shock wave loosened the restaurant's ceiling tiles and buckled the floors. As documented in videos from two amateur photographers, smoke built with terrifying speed in the penthouse dining room, cascading thicker from the window seams here than from those on the floors closer to the impact. Doris Eng and the conference coordinators tried to maintain order, but panic and confusion quickly spread. Ironically, many in the crowd made their living providing information or serving the equipment that carried it. Risk Waters had invited high-flying communications experts to speak at the conference. But with thickening smoke and no power, the restaurant was fast becoming an isolation zone. Everyone scrambled for scraps of news. Stephen Tompsett, senior vice president of corporate technology for Instinet Corporation, a leading electronic stockbroker, instructed his wife by email to watch CNN and send updates. *What was happening? Was it another bombing?* The answer came at 9:03 A.M., special delivery.

United Airlines Flight 165 hit the South Tower and within less than an hour the building imploded. At this point, the trapped guests and staff must have known they were doomed. Christine Olender, Windows assistant general manager, phoned Port Authority police four times, begging for help. Adored by the immigrant staff, who called her their "Yankee Doodle sweetheart" because she had been born on the Fourth of July, the normally perky Chicago native was frantic.

"We're getting no direction up here!" she told Officer Steve Maggett. "Right now we need to find a safe haven on 106—where the smoke condition isn't bad."

"We'll send a rescue crew up as soon as possible," Murray said.

"What's your ETA?" Olender asked.

"As soon as possible," Murray repeated. "As soon as humanly possible."

That wasn't good enough.

"Things are rapidly getting worse," Olender said. "We . . . we have . . . the fresh air is going down fast! I'm not exaggerating," she added.

"Ma'am," Murray assured her, "I know you're not exaggerating."

With the stairway blocked and the smoke and flames rising, some couldn't wait. The jumper in the news photo "The Falling Man" is probably sound engineer Jonathan Briley. But most said farewell to their loved ones. They emailed from laptops, texted from PalmPilots, or used the restaurant fax. The transmitter on the roof sustained the mobile phone network until the last minute, despite the deluge of calls from downtown. The sardonic joked it was the first time Verizon Wireless had never dropped a call.

At 10:28 A.M., the North Tower collapsed. The 360-foot antenna and a dozen broadcast offices crashed through the ceiling and crushed the restaurant's seventy-three employees and a Muslim security guard. Six more workers building a new wine cellar in the basement were buried alive under the rubble. Nothing remains of Windows on the World except a menu, a uniform, some china, a champagne glass, and a grill scraper, preserved at the Smithsonian like artifacts from Pompeii.

THE WTC ATTACKS and the resulting recession devastated New York's low-wage and largely immigrant hospitality industry. Citywide, over thirteen thousand restaurant workers were displaced, including two hundred and fifty from Windows on the World. The families of the fallen went begging. Using actuary tables, Kenneth Feinberg, Special Master of the September 11 Victim Compensation Fund, patiently explained why the life of a Dominican dishwasher was worth only a tenth as much as a Wharton Business School graduate's. Hotel and Restaurant Employees Local 100 raised relief money but would not assist the nonunion workers who comprise ninety percent of New York's restaurant workforce. Accordingly, two former Windows on the World employees, Fekkak Mamdouh and Shulaika La Cruz, established an advocacy group, Restaurant Opportunities Center of New York (ROC-NY).

The immigrants thought this measure was temporary. Like a cargo cult, they expected Windows on the World to rise from the ashes. Owner David Emil had vowed to rebuild the restaurant and to rehire its staff, but despite press conferences and come-hither offers from Marriott, it never happened. In fact, when he opened Noche, a Times Square restaurant and nightclub described by one reviewer as "Ricky Ricardo on steroids," an outraged Emil showed ex-employees the door. These ingrates actually wanted a union! Bowing to curbside protests and bad press, Emil hired thirty-five of his old crew. The rest started Colors, a cooperative restaurant honoring the memory of their dead comrades.

Located on Lafayette Street near Astor Place, between Greenwich Village and the East Village, Colors reflects the diversity of its owners. At the January 6, 2006, opening, *Wall Street Journal* subscribers feasted on ceviche, avocado soup, mango pepper citronette, and panko-crusted tofu. Global capitalism, they toasted, had found a silver lining in the cloud of Ground Zero. But within a year, the publicity and goodwill faded, and the co-op's idealism collided with a crowded and competitive market, where seventy percent of New York's twenty-six thousand restaurants close or change hands within their first five years of business.

"The place just stopped making money," admits Jean Emy Pierre, once line cook at Windows on the World, now executive chef at Colors. "We're dead, doing ten, twenty, thirty covers a night," he sighs, referring to the number of customers. "That was the point where I was like, 'What's going on? Why aren't people coming? What did we do wrong?'"

WINDOWS' FORMER blue-chip clients do not patronize Colors for auld lang syne. Instead, pining for the glory days, when the price of gold and oil soared even on 9/11, they mourn and name-drop on the WOTW memorial website. Meanwhile, the market has suffered the worst meltdown since the Great Depression. After publishing a chortling autobiography, in which he admits that his Delphic pronouncements during the boom years were gobbledy-gook, ex–Federal Reserve Chairman Alan Greenspan practically wept before Congress: "Those of us who have looked to the self-interest of lending institutions to protect shareholders' equity are in a state of shocked disbelief."

As for me, I teach business writing in an upstate Rust Belt, can't afford to take my wife to the local Italian restaurant, rarely visit Manhattan, and avoid Wall Street. Downtown makes me ill. Grief, my father suggests over dinner. I'm still mourning the colleagues I lost nine years ago. Airborne toxins, an EPA buddy explains, sharing a sub. Ground Zero remains peppered with carcinogens, even if the government claims otherwise. They both may be right, of course; but I have my own explanation.

ACKNOWLEDGMENTS

LIKE *TRIPPA ALLA ROMANA,* this collection resulted from long simmering. Over the years, earlier versions of these essays have appeared in various literary journals.

The following list of acknowledgments is arranged chronologically:

"Exiles from Cockaigne" in *River Styx 49: History and the Perfect Past* (Summer 1997)

"Coffeehouse Philosophy" in *River Styx* 52 (Spring 1998)

"Tears and Onions" in *River Styx: 25th Anniversary Issue* 58/59 (Fall 2000)

"Aperitif" in *Alimentum: The Literature of Food* 5 (Winter 2005)

"A Load of Tripe" in *Voices in Italian Americana* 15.2 (Spring 2006)

"Lucullan Feasts" in *River Styx: A Readable Feast* 76 (Summer 2008)

"Lunch with Trimalchio" in *The Normal School: A Literary Magazine* 1 (Fall 2008)

"Dark Chocolate" in *Voices in Italian Americana* 19.2 (Fall 2008)

"Top of the World" in *Essays & Fictions* V.V (October 2009)

"Bitter Greens" in *Alimentum: The Literature of Food* 9 (Summer 2010)

I thank editors Sophie Beck, Steven Church, Fred Gardaphe, Paolo Giordano, Joshua Land, Paulette Licitra, Chiara Mazzucchelli, Richard Newman, David Pollock, Matt Roberts, Peter Selgin, Anthony Tamburri, and Danielle Winterton for allowing me to reprint these essays and for urging me to publish this book.

Who says too many cooks spoil the broth?